Introduction

As parents and educators, we recognize the pivotal role mathematics plays in shaping a child's academic journey and future success. Yet, the path to mathematical proficiency can often seem daunting, fraught with challenges and complexities. That's where the transformative power of MathFlare Workbooks shine through, illuminating the way forward with clarity, precision, and purpose.

Introducing MathFlare Workbooks – a beacon of guidance, a testament to excellence, and a catalyst for achievement. Crafted with meticulous care and expertise, MathFlare Workbooks stand as paragons of educational excellence, designed to nurture young minds, ignite a passion for learning, and develop a deep-rooted understanding of mathematical concepts.

Picture this: your child eagerly delves into the pages of Mathflare Workbook, greeted by a step-by-step guide illuminated with vivid examples that demystify complex mathematical concepts. With each turn of the page, they embark on a journey of discovery, encountering thoughtfully curated practice questions that reinforce learning and hone problem-solving skills. And when they unveil the answers to those very questions, a sense of accomplishment blossoms within them – a tangible reward for their hard work and dedication.

But MathFlare Workbooks are more than just tools for learning; they are pathways to comprehension, fostering a deep-seated understanding of mathematical concepts through a sequential, logical flow. From fundamental principles to advanced problem-solving strategies, every chapter builds upon the last, ensuring a robust foundation upon which future knowledge can be constructed.

As parents, we yearn for nothing more than to see our children thrive, to witness the spark of inspiration ignited within them as they conquer academic challenges with confidence and poise. MathFlare Workbooks serve as partners in this noble endeavor, offering not just practice questions, but the keys to unlocking a world of opportunity.

And for teachers, MathFlare Workbooks stand as invaluable allies in the quest to cultivate mathematical proficiency in the classroom. With answers readily available, instructors can focus on guiding and nurturing their students, confident in the knowledge that MathFlare Workbooks provide a solid framework upon which to build.

In the pages of MathFlare Workbooks, we find not just the promise of academic excellence, but the seeds of a brighter tomorrow. So let us embrace the power of mathematics, let us champion the journey of learning, and let us pave the way for a generation of young minds poised to shape the world. With MathFlare Workbooks as our guide, the possibilities are infinite, and the future, bright.

Table of Contents

MathFlare
MATH WORKBOOK
Grade 2
Step by Step Guide and Essential Practice with Answers
Addition Subtraction
Multiplication
Place Value and Expanded Notations
Geometry
MathFlare Publishing

MathFlare
MATH WORKBOOK
Grade 2-3
Step by Step Guide and Essential Practice with Answers
Addition Subtraction
Multiplication and Division
Place Value and Expanded Notations
Geometry
MathFlare Publishing

MathFlare
MATH WORKBOOK
Grade 3
Step by Step Guide and Essential Practice with Answers
Multiplication and Division
Decimals
Place Value and Expanded Notations
Fractions and Geometry
MathFlare Publishing

MathFlare
MATH WORKBOOK
Grade 1
Step by Step Guide and Essential Practice with Answers
Counting and Numbers
Addition and Subtraction
Place Value and Expanded Notations
Understanding Time
MathFlare Publishing

MathFlare
MATH WORKBOOK
Grade 1-2
Step by Step Guide and Essential Practice with Answers
Counting and Numbers
Addition and Subtraction
Place Value and Expanded Notations
Understanding Time
MathFlare Publishing

MathFlare
MATH WORKBOOK
Grade 3-4
Step by Step Guide and Essential Practice with Answers
Addition Subtraction
Multiplication Division
Place Value and Expanded Notations
Fractions and Geometry
MathFlare Publishing

MathFlare
MATH WORKBOOK
Grade 4
Step by Step Guide and Essential Practice with Answers
Addition Subtraction
Multiplication Division
Place Value and Expanded Notations
Fractions and Geometry
MathFlare Publishing

MathFlare
MATH WORKBOOK
Grade 4-5
Step by Step Guide and Essential Practice with Answers
Multiplication Division
Place Value and Expanded Notations
Fractions and Geometry
Unit Conversion
MathFlare Publishing

Addition and Subtraction

Addition

Adding is like putting things together to see how many we have altogether.

For instance, imagine we have 2 colorful blocks. Then, we add 3 more blocks. How many blocks do we have in total?

Let's count them together. 1, 2, 3, 4, 5.

Exactly! We have 5 blocks altogether! We show this with a plus sign (+) like this:

$$2 + 3 = 5.$$

Now, let's try another one.

If we have 1 pencil and we add one more pencil, how many pencils do we have in total?

Right, we have 2 pencils! We can write it down like this:

$$1 + 1 = 2.$$

Let's solve a problem:

$$\begin{array}{r} 17 \\ +\ 3 \\ \hline 20 \end{array}$$

Subtraction

Subtraction is all about taking things away or finding out how much is left.

Imagine you have a basket of 5 apples. Now, let's pretend you ate 2 of those yummy apples. How many do you have left?

Let's count them together. 1, 2, 3. Yes, you got it! You have 3 apples left!

We use this special sign "-" to show that we're taking away some apples.

Now, let's try another one! Imagine you have a bag full of 8 colorful marbles. Now, let's say you give away 3 of them to your friend. How many marbles are still in your bag?

Let's count them together. 1, 2, 3, 4, 5. Yes, you're correct! You have 5 marbles left!

We can write it down like this: 8 - 3 = 5.

Subtraction helps us figure out what's left after we take some away.

Let's solve a problem:

$$\begin{array}{r} 18 \\ -\ 16 \\ \hline 2 \end{array}$$

Commutative Property of Addition

The commutative property of addition tells us that it doesn't matter which order we add numbers together; we'll still get the same answer.

For instance: you have 3 blue blocks and 2 red blocks.

Now, if we add them together, we get 5 blocks total, right? 3 (blue) + 2 (red) = 5.

But guess what? We can also add them in a different order!

Let's try adding the red blocks first, then the blue ones.

So, we have 2 (red) + 3 (blue).

Let's count them together. 1, 2, 3, 4, 5. We still get 5 blocks in total!

It doesn't matter if we add the blue blocks first or the red ones first, we still end up with the same number of blocks.

Word Problems

Word problems are like little puzzles that help us use addition in real-life situations.

For instance:

1. Jake has 6 carrots. He gets 2 more carrots. How many carrots does he have now?

To find out how many carrots he has now, we add the number of carrots he started with (6) to the number of carrots he got (2).

So, we add 6 + 2, which equals 8.

Jake now has 8 carrots in total!

2. Jake saved up 4 dollars to buy pencils. He spent 2 dollars on it. How much money does he have left?

To solve this problem, we need to start with the number of dollars Jake started with and subtract the number of dollars he spent on the pencils.

So, we subtract 2 from 4, which equals 2:

Jake has 2 dollars left after buying the pencils.

We need to understand what the problem is asking and what information it provides. Then, we can use addition or subtraction, depending on whether we're combining or taking away objects, to find the answer.

Let's solve problems from the exercises:

There are 5 brushes on the shelf. Genesis puts 1 more brush on   the shelf. How
many brushes are there on the shelf now?

$$
\begin{array}{r}
5 \\
+\,1 \\
\hline
6
\end{array}
$$

5 five brushes on the shelf
+ 1 Genesis Put one more
6 There are 6 brushes on the shelf now

Emma has 9 dresses. She gave 1 dress to Stephanie. How many   dresses does
Emma have now?

9 Emma has 9 dresses
-1 She gave away 1 dress
8
Emma has 8 dresses left

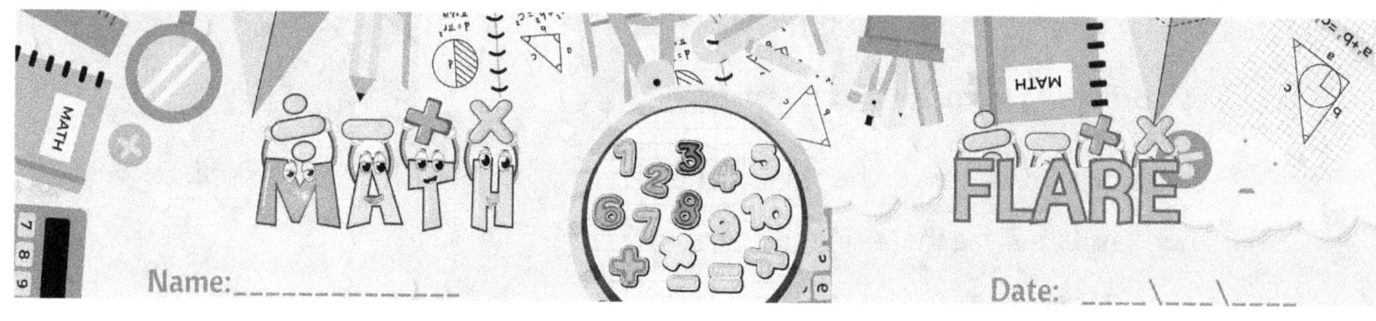

Addition 1 through 20

Find the Sum.

1. 15 + 7	2. 10 + 17	3. 18 + 4	4. 5 + 13	5. 11 + 2
6. 13 + 6	7. 10 + 9	8. 16 + 19	9. 8 + 20	10. 20 + 6
11. 7 + 12	12. 15 + 8	13. 1 + 17	14. 19 + 11	15. 6 + 1
16. 11 + 16	17. 13 + 9	18. 7 + 20	19. 12 + 15	20. 18 + 7
21. 6 + 2	22. 1 + 19	23. 19 + 9	24. 17 + 8	25. 16 + 18

26. 9 + 5	27. 6 + 5	28. 16 + 4	29. 12 + 4	30. 17 + 2
31. 6 + 15	32. 8 + 11	33. 11 + 17	34. 13 + 1	35. 3 + 17
36. 8 + 12	37. 3 + 14	38. 1 + 6	39. 12 + 17	40. 9 + 13
41. 2 + 12	42. 14 + 8	43. 12 + 7	44. 11 + 9	45. 13 + 4
46. 9 + 10	47. 18 + 17	48. 14 + 11	49. 9 + 3	50. 16 + 16

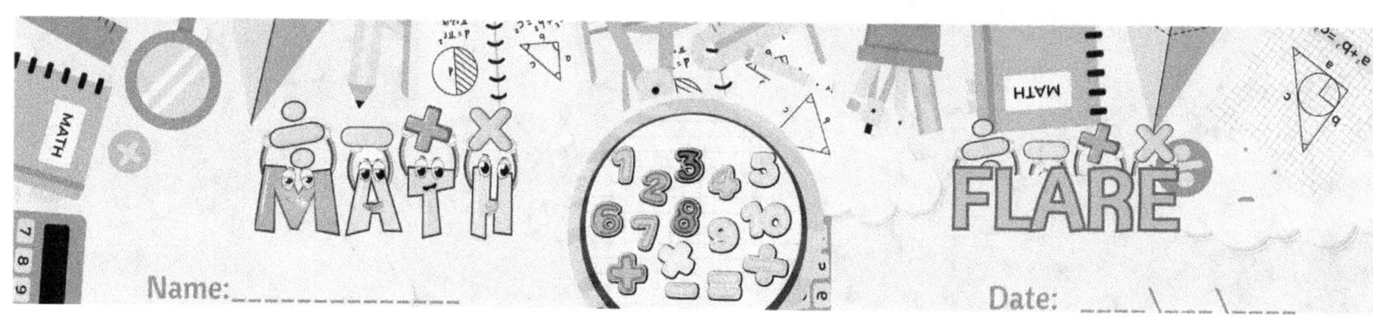

51. 6 + 20	52. 3 + 12	53. 5 + 11	54. 15 + 5	55. 1 + 14
56. 1 + 20	57. 19 + 4	58. 6 + 4	59. 8 + 19	60. 9 + 18
61. 14 + 6	62. 13 + 10	63. 12 + 2	64. 9 + 7	65. 17 + 5
66. 7 + 14	67. 17 + 16	68. 6 + 3	69. 12 + 14	70. 15 + 14
71. 16 + 8	72. 11 + 14	73. 12 + 6	74. 17 + 12	75. 12 + 13

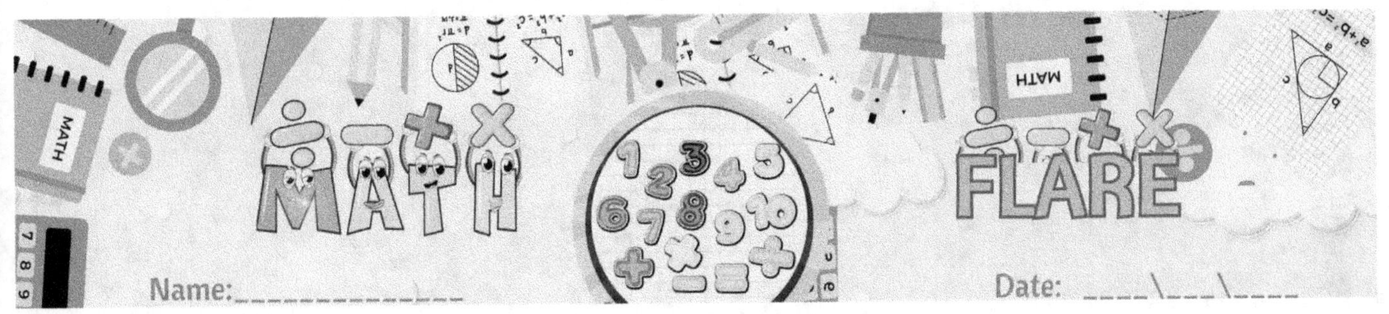

76. 4 + 16	77. 19 + 15	78. 20 + 11	79. 8 + 9	80. 9 + 16
81. 3 + 4	82. 19 + 6	83. 8 + 15	84. 4 + 1	85. 10 + 6
86. 18 + 18	87. 10 + 4	88. 10 + 5	89. 3 + 5	90. 2 + 11
91. 4 + 2	92. 7 + 7	93. 12 + 9	94. 14 + 4	95. 20 + 17
96. 11 + 3	97. 17 + 3	98. 2 + 5	99. 20 + 9	100. 4 + 18

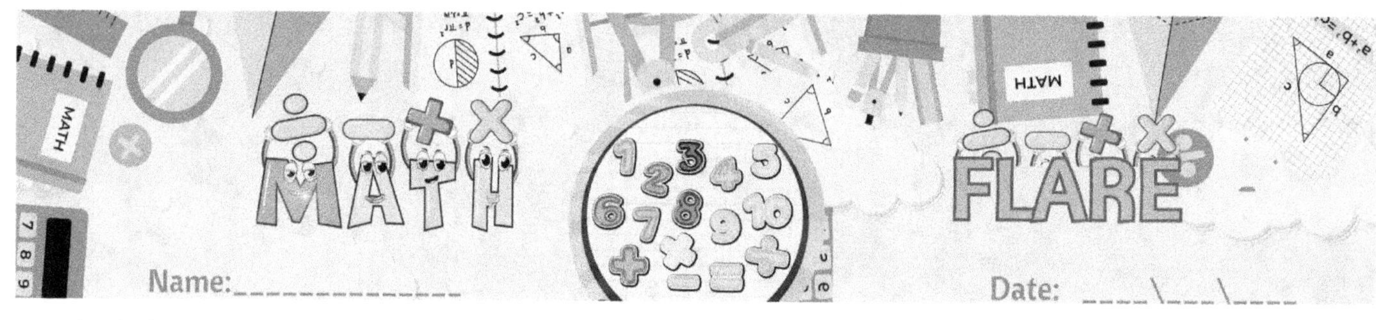

Addition 1 through 20

Find the unknown number.

101. $3 + 8 = \underline{\quad}$

102. $7 + 10 = \underline{\quad}$

103. $\underline{\quad} + 7 = 22$

104. $13 + 7 = \underline{\quad}$

105. $\underline{\quad} + 5 = 23$

106. $15 + \underline{\quad} = 30$

107. $17 + 8 = \underline{\quad}$

108. $4 + 11 = \underline{\quad}$

109. $16 + 17 = \underline{\quad}$

110. $12 + \underline{\quad} = 28$

111. $10 + 18 = \underline{\quad}$

112. $8 + 9 = \underline{\quad}$

113. $2 + 15 = \underline{\quad}$

114. $11 + \underline{\quad} = 12$

115. $19 + 19 = \underline{\quad}$

116. $20 + \underline{\quad} = 25$

117. $\underline{\quad} + 3 = 20$

118. $\underline{\quad} + 1 = 15$

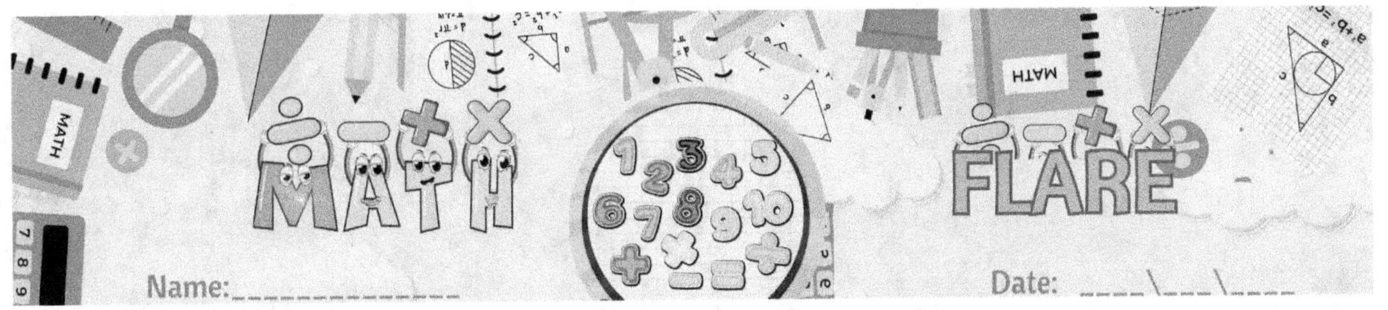

119. ___ + 4 = 17

120. 16 + 4 = ___

121. ___ + 11 = 23

122. ___ + 12 = 18

123. 6 + ___ = 11

124. 17 + ___ = 35

125. ___ + 15 = 32

126. ___ + 8 = 22

127. 6 + ___ = 15

128. 15 + 5 = ___

129. ___ + 2 = 12

130. 15 + ___ = 27

131. ___ + 19 = 27

132. 6 + ___ = 17

133. 17 + ___ = 33

134. 14 + ___ = 17

135. 18 + 13 = ___

136. 2 + ___ = 11

137. 6 + ___ = 25

138. 14 + 16 = ___

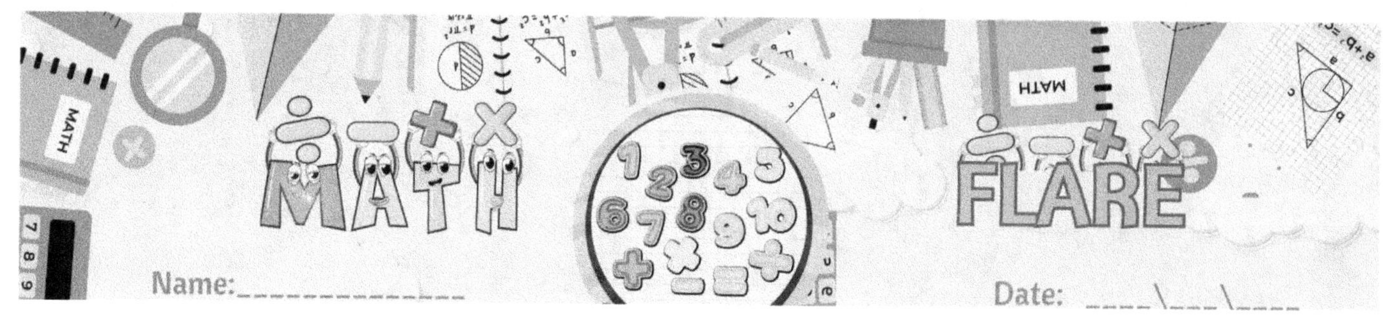

139. $4 + \underline{\quad} = 20$

140. $4 + 6 = \underline{\quad}$

141. $\underline{\quad} + 12 = 19$

142. $\underline{\quad} + 9 = 28$

143. $\underline{\quad} + 10 = 18$

144. $9 + 19 = \underline{\quad}$

145. $\underline{\quad} + 7 = 11$

146. $\underline{\quad} + 14 = 21$

147. $8 + 2 = \underline{\quad}$

148. $6 + \underline{\quad} = 21$

149. $17 + \underline{\quad} = 19$

150. $\underline{\quad} + 17 = 24$

151. $\underline{\quad} + 4 = 15$

152. $16 + \underline{\quad} = 30$

153. $3 + 3 = \underline{\quad}$

154. $\underline{\quad} + 3 = 12$

155. $13 + 13 = \underline{\quad}$

156. $12 + 9 = \underline{\quad}$

157. $9 + \underline{\quad} = 14$

158. $3 + 4 = \underline{\quad}$

159. 18 + ___ = 25

160. ___ + 6 = 8

161. 16 + 8 = ___

162. ___ + 10 = 20

163. 9 + 18 = ___

164. 9 + ___ = 19

165. ___ + 6 = 15

166. ___ + 4 = 10

167. 18 + ___ = 36

168. 19 + ___ = 21

169. 12 + ___ = 14

170. ___ + 14 = 28

171. 3 + 19 = ___

172. ___ + 14 = 27

173. 4 + ___ = 5

174. ___ + 18 = 34

175. 2 + ___ = 7

176. ___ + 7 = 21

177. ___ + 6 = 11

178. 14 + ___ = 33

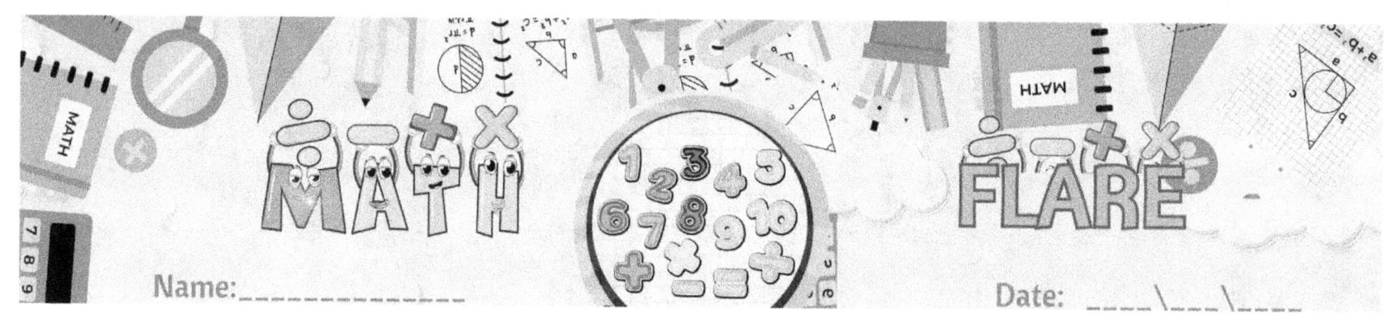

179. $4 + \underline{} = 22$

180. $\underline{} + 17 = 22$

181. $\underline{} + 15 = 29$

182. $15 + 14 = \underline{}$

183. $\underline{} + 16 = 29$

184. $6 + 8 = \underline{}$

185. $\underline{} + 6 = 9$

186. $8 + 8 = \underline{}$

187. $10 + \underline{} = 25$

188. $\underline{} + 13 = 17$

189. $8 + 7 = \underline{}$

190. $\underline{} + 9 = 25$

191. $\underline{} + 7 = 17$

192. $7 + 2 = \underline{}$

193. $\underline{} + 19 = 30$

194. $19 + \underline{} = 34$

195. $\underline{} + 8 = 28$

196. $\underline{} + 3 = 9$

197. $3 + \underline{} = 19$

198. $9 + \underline{} = 21$

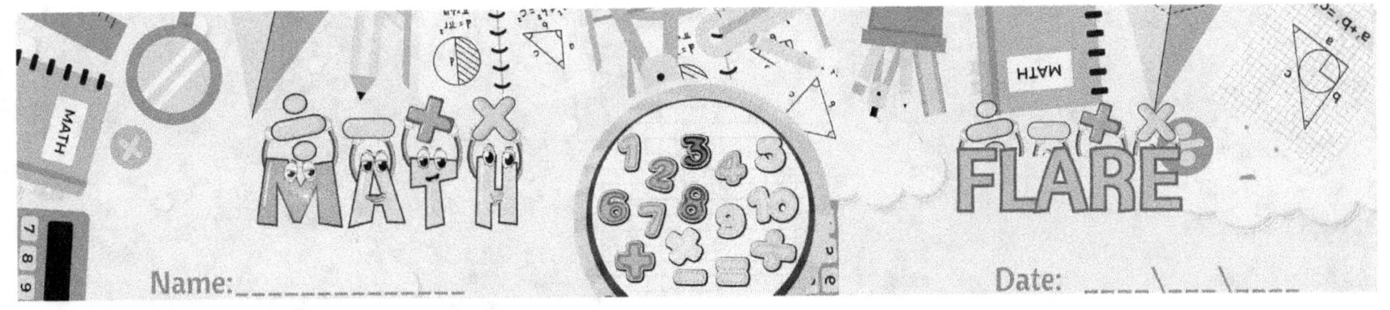

Addition 1 through 50

Find the Sum.

199. 3 + 27	200. 3 + 16	201. 7 + 6	202. 18 + 18	203. 22 + 34
204. 35 + 30	205. 29 + 21	206. 13 + 40	207. 47 + 16	208. 11 + 9
209. 9 + 12	210. 35 + 4	211. 20 + 14	212. 26 + 21	213. 3 + 13
214. 29 + 2	215. 14 + 12	216. 20 + 48	217. 14 + 2	218. 47 + 4

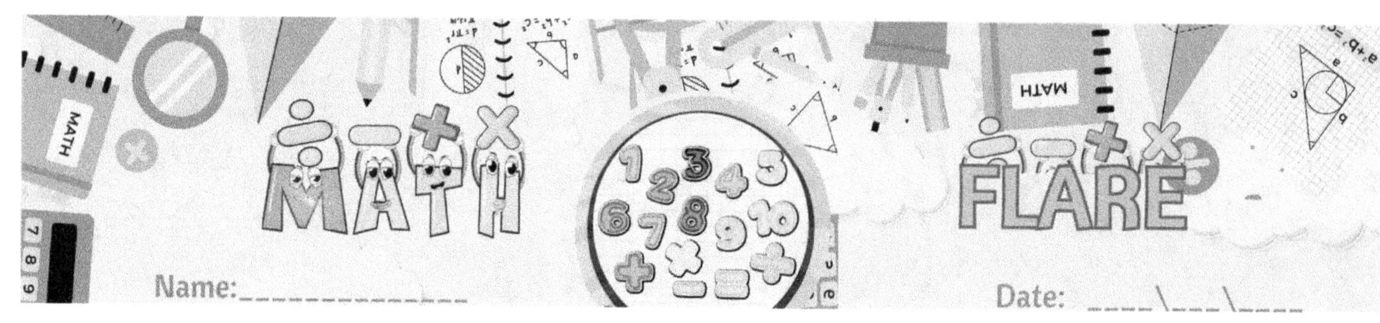

219. 50 + 11	220. 26 + 15	221. 4 + 20	222. 39 + 36	223. 36 + 24
224. 9 + 40	225. 29 + 13	226. 20 + 40	227. 42 + 49	228. 46 + 43
229. 30 + 47	230. 15 + 11	231. 7 + 34	232. 17 + 18	233. 1 + 15
234. 27 + 45	235. 19 + 8	236. 9 + 48	237. 37 + 22	238. 49 + 1
239. 24 + 40	240. 34 + 29	241. 5 + 39	242. 23 + 2	243. 42 + 30

244. 7 + 15 ———	245. 6 + 4 ———	246. 25 + 4 ———	247. 46 + 16 ———	248. 9 + 20 ———
249. 4 + 22 ———	250. 35 + 23 ———	251. 47 + 13 ———	252. 22 + 22 ———	253. 5 + 22 ———
254. 4 + 21 ———	255. 50 + 46 ———	256. 20 + 39 ———	257. 14 + 36 ———	258. 7 + 18 ———
259. 12 + 16 ———	260. 27 + 21 ———	261. 8 + 13 ———	262. 41 + 16 ———	263. 33 + 6 ———
264. 3 + 22 ———	265. 14 + 30 ———	266. 48 + 3 ———	267. 6 + 12 ———	268. 32 + 41 ———

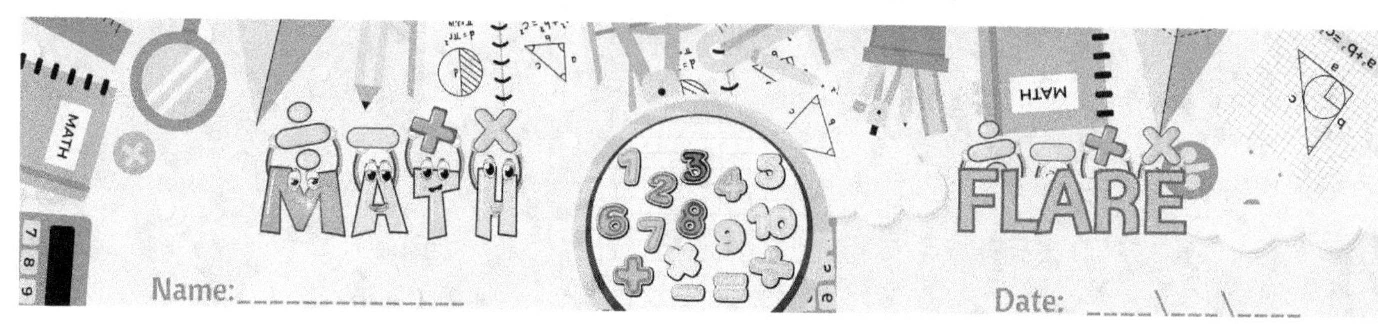

269. 18 + 2	270. 46 + 20	271. 27 + 36	272. 16 + 10	273. 34 + 35
274. 40 + 11	275. 9 + 41	276. 9 + 38	277. 46 + 15	278. 15 + 35
279. 23 + 7	280. 38 + 49	281. 20 + 32	282. 8 + 20	283. 48 + 18
284. 34 + 3	285. 5 + 16	286. 50 + 10	287. 20 + 7	288. 44 + 23
289. 47 + 32	290. 31 + 48	291. 17 + 41	292. 14 + 23	293. 22 + 11

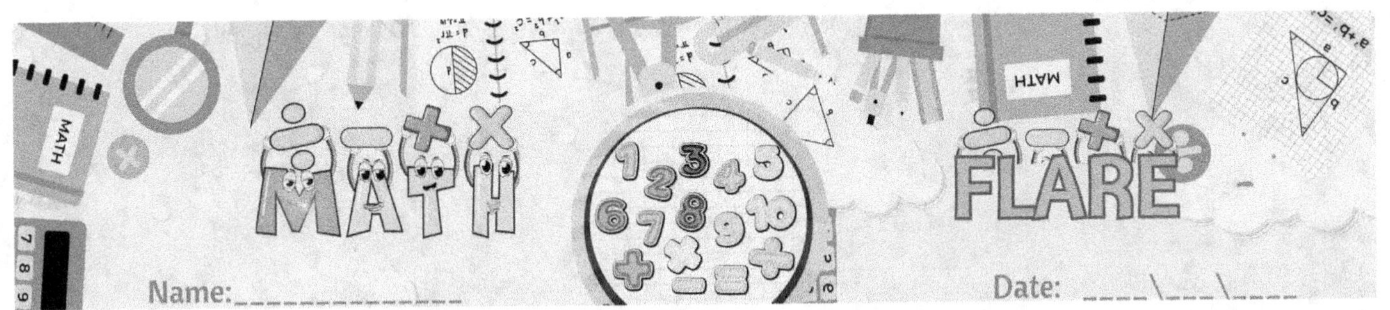

294. 7 + 41	295. 47 + 47	296. 19 + 12	297. 14 + 47	298. 1 + 45
299. 29 + 45	300. 12 + 17	301. 2 + 38	302. 7 + 43	303. 41 + 49
304. 19 + 39	305. 21 + 43	306. 38 + 41	307. 26 + 40	308. 33 + 29
309. 20 + 36	310. 49 + 38	311. 12 + 43	312. 6 + 8	313. 47 + 39
314. 46 + 22	315. 7 + 49	316. 44 + 3	317. 21 + 15	318. 47 + 29

Subtraction 1 through 20

Find the Difference.

319.	320.	321.	322.	323.
12 − 11	2 − 1	1 − 1	17 − 12	11 − 3

324.	325.	326.	327.	328.
15 − 7	19 − 14	4 − 2	10 − 5	16 − 2

329.	330.	331.	332.	333.
11 − 10	19 − 16	12 − 2	14 − 4	8 − 4

334.	335.	336.	337.	338.
4 − 3	2 − 2	9 − 4	7 − 6	10 − 8

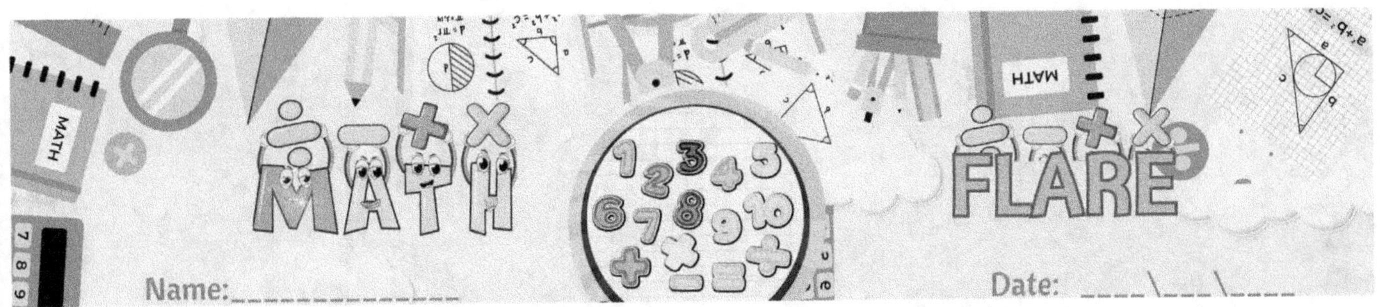

339. 5 − 4	340. 4 − 4	341. 19 − 5	342. 19 − 15	343. 6 − 4
344. 17 − 17	345. 3 − 1	346. 12 − 9	347. 16 − 5	348. 6 − 3
349. 14 − 11	350. 8 − 5	351. 16 − 12	352. 18 − 2	353. 14 − 9
354. 8 − 3	355. 7 − 2	356. 11 − 5	357. 11 − 2	358. 17 − 4
359. 16 − 10	360. 16 − 3	361. 19 − 18	362. 12 − 10	363. 6 − 6

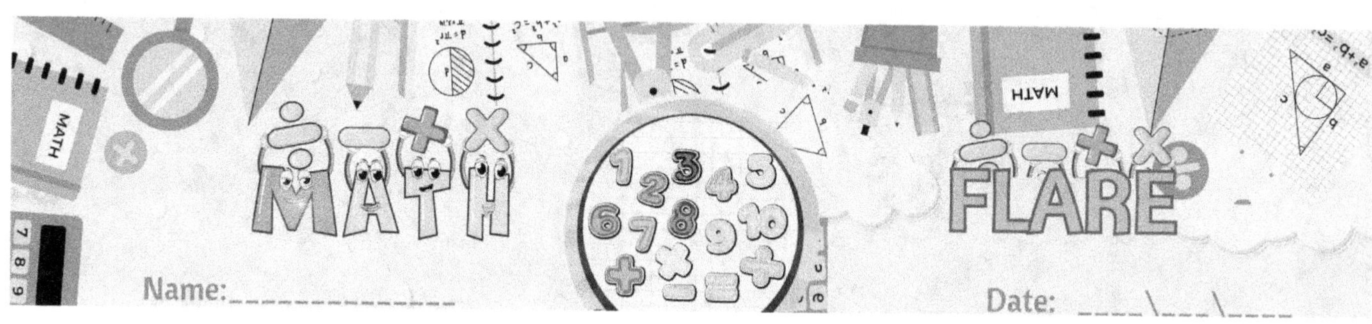

364. $\begin{array}{r} 5 \\ -\ 3 \\ \hline \end{array}$	365. $\begin{array}{r} 8 \\ -\ 7 \\ \hline \end{array}$	366. $\begin{array}{r} 15 \\ -\ 13 \\ \hline \end{array}$	367. $\begin{array}{r} 20 \\ -\ 6 \\ \hline \end{array}$	368. $\begin{array}{r} 14 \\ -\ 12 \\ \hline \end{array}$
369. $\begin{array}{r} 13 \\ -\ 4 \\ \hline \end{array}$	370. $\begin{array}{r} 19 \\ -\ 6 \\ \hline \end{array}$	371. $\begin{array}{r} 9 \\ -\ 8 \\ \hline \end{array}$	372. $\begin{array}{r} 20 \\ -\ 20 \\ \hline \end{array}$	373. $\begin{array}{r} 20 \\ -\ 17 \\ \hline \end{array}$
374. $\begin{array}{r} 17 \\ -\ 1 \\ \hline \end{array}$	375. $\begin{array}{r} 15 \\ -\ 12 \\ \hline \end{array}$	376. $\begin{array}{r} 15 \\ -\ 5 \\ \hline \end{array}$	377. $\begin{array}{r} 18 \\ -\ 14 \\ \hline \end{array}$	378. $\begin{array}{r} 12 \\ -\ 12 \\ \hline \end{array}$
379. $\begin{array}{r} 11 \\ -\ 8 \\ \hline \end{array}$	380. $\begin{array}{r} 12 \\ -\ 1 \\ \hline \end{array}$	381. $\begin{array}{r} 13 \\ -\ 3 \\ \hline \end{array}$	382. $\begin{array}{r} 3 \\ -\ 2 \\ \hline \end{array}$	383. $\begin{array}{r} 19 \\ -\ 7 \\ \hline \end{array}$
384. $\begin{array}{r} 13 \\ -\ 6 \\ \hline \end{array}$	385. $\begin{array}{r} 5 \\ -\ 2 \\ \hline \end{array}$	386. $\begin{array}{r} 17 \\ -\ 14 \\ \hline \end{array}$	387. $\begin{array}{r} 8 \\ -\ 1 \\ \hline \end{array}$	388. $\begin{array}{r} 12 \\ -\ 6 \\ \hline \end{array}$

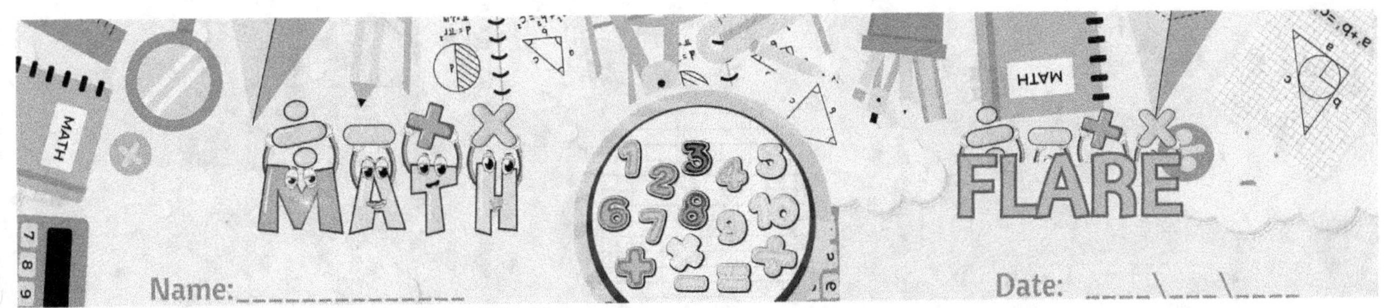

389. 18 − 9	390. 15 − 10	391. 11 − 9	392. 15 − 4	393. 8 − 2
394. 19 − 19	395. 13 − 12	396. 19 − 17	397. 9 − 5	398. 12 − 4
399. 10 − 9	400. 9 − 2	401. 17 − 10	402. 5 − 1	403. 15 − 3
404. 17 − 6	405. 15 − 15	406. 13 − 11	407. 10 − 4	408. 16 − 4
409. 9 − 6	410. 12 − 7	411. 6 − 1	412. 7 − 3	413. 11 − 7

MathFlare - Addition and Subtraction 1st and 2nd Grade

18

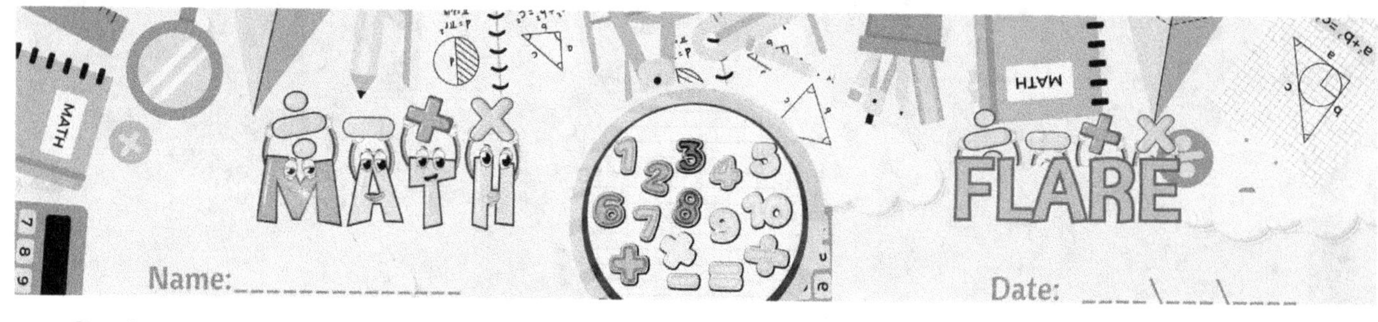

Subtraction 1 through 20

Find the unknown number.

414. ___ − 7 = 1

415. ___ − 5 = 2

416. 7 − 4 = ___

417. 18 − ___ = 11

418. 5 − ___ = 3

419. 9 − ___ = 4

420. 13 − 5 = ___

421. 17 − 6 = ___

422. 14 − ___ = 5

423. 1 − ___ = 0

424. 19 − ___ = 12

425. ___ − 1 = 2

426. 15 − 11 = ___

427. 6 − 1 = ___

428. 17 − ___ = 16

429. 14 − ___ = 9

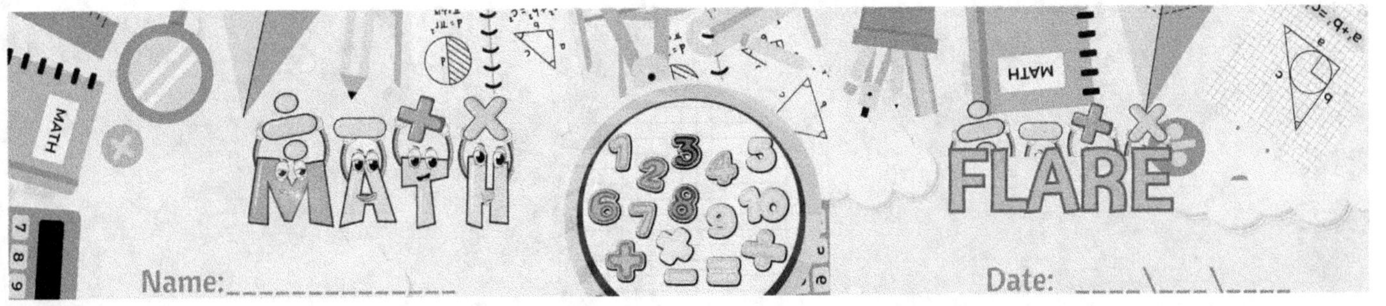

430. ___ - 2 = 0

431. ___ - 8 = 3

432. ___ - 2 = 13

433. ___ - 7 = 3

434. ___ - 2 = 16

435. ___ - 7 = 0

436. 18 - 14 = ___

437. 18 - ___ = 9

438. 16 - ___ = 0

439. 10 - 8 = ___

440. 12 - ___ = 5

441. ___ - 3 = 16

442. ___ - 5 = 6

443. 7 - 3 = ___

444. 18 - ___ = 1

445. ___ - 13 = 3

446. 14 - ___ = 12

447. 16 - 4 = ___

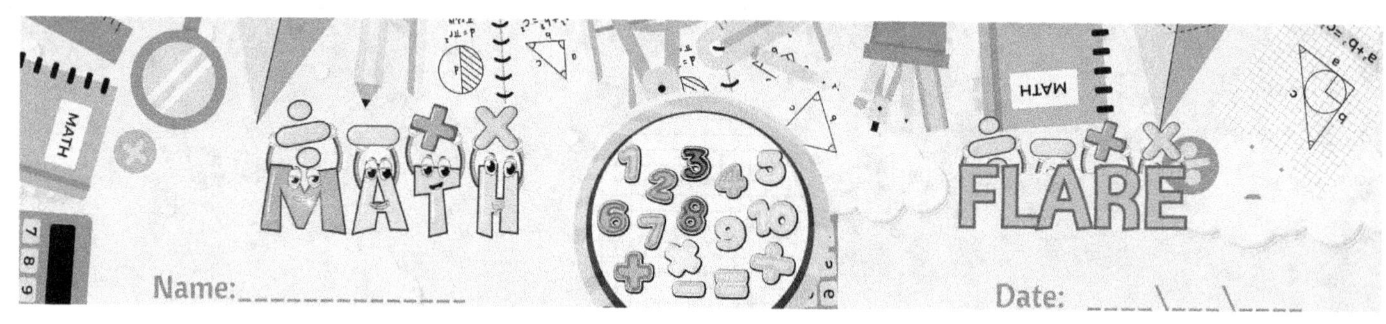

448. $16 - \underline{\quad} = 2$

449. $3 - \underline{\quad} = 1$

450. $10 - 3 = \underline{\quad}$

451. $\underline{\quad} - 2 = 8$

452. $4 - 3 = \underline{\quad}$

453. $4 - \underline{\quad} = 2$

454. $\underline{\quad} - 4 = 0$

455. $13 - 8 = \underline{\quad}$

456. $7 - \underline{\quad} = 5$

457. $2 - 1 = \underline{\quad}$

458. $13 - 1 = \underline{\quad}$

459. $14 - 14 = \underline{\quad}$

460. $8 - 5 = \underline{\quad}$

461. $\underline{\quad} - 6 = 1$

462. $16 - \underline{\quad} = 10$

463. $19 - \underline{\quad} = 13$

464. $\underline{\quad} - 11 = 5$

465. $19 - \underline{\quad} = 15$

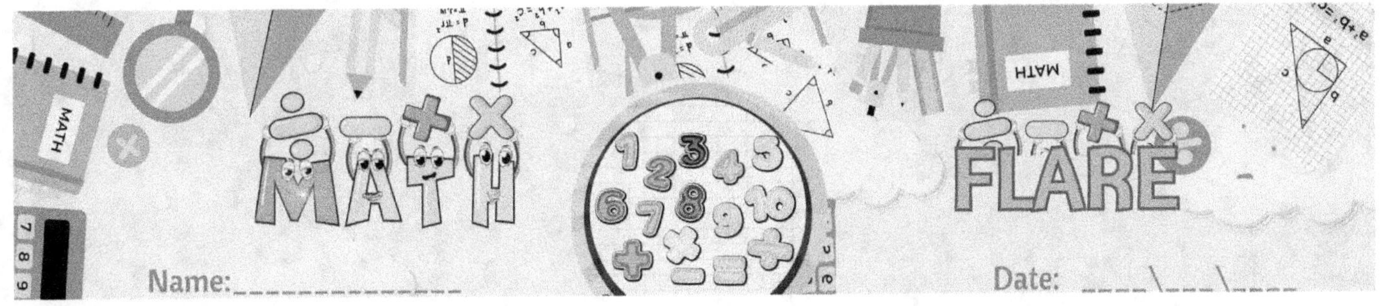

466. 11 - ___ = 5

467. 13 - 7 = ___

468. 9 - ___ = 7

469. 13 - 9 = ___

470. ___ - 5 = 5

471. ___ - 1 = 11

472. ___ - 7 = 2

473. 6 - 4 = ___

474. ___ - 17 = 0

475. 17 - ___ = 6

476. 9 - ___ = 6

477. 6 - 5 = ___

478. ___ - 3 = 11

479. ___ - 3 = 5

480. 15 - ___ = 6

481. ___ - 3 = 10

482. 6 - ___ = 4

483. 8 - 6 = ___

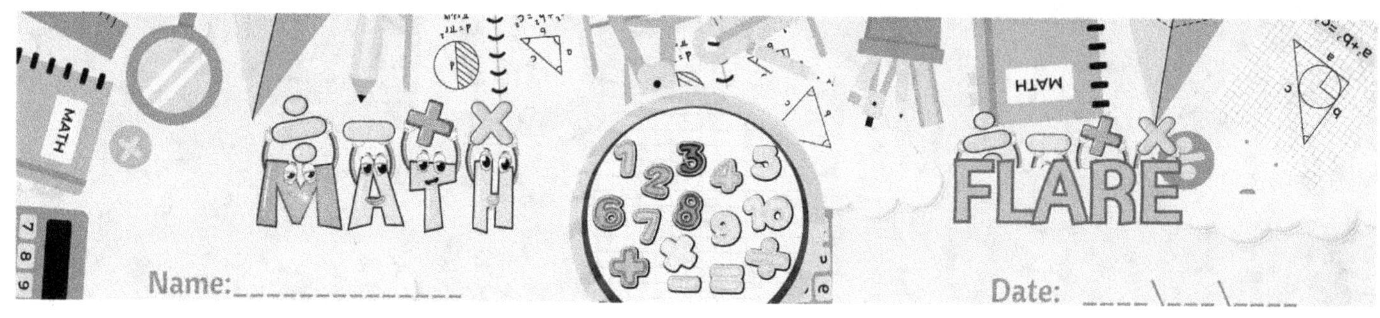

484. 6 - 3 = ___

485. 13 - 6 = ___

486. ___ - 1 = 6

487. 20 - ___ = 5

488. 17 - 9 = ___

489. 12 - ___ = 10

490. 11 - 1 = ___

491. ___ - 5 = 7

492. 4 - 1 = ___

493. 19 - ___ = 2

494. 19 - 8 = ___

495. 10 - ___ = 4

496. 17 - 16 = ___

497. 5 - 3 = ___

498. 14 - 13 = ___

499. 8 - 4 = ___

500. 20 - ___ = 4

501. 17 - 5 = ___

502. ___ - 1 = 4

503. 15 - ___ = 8

504. 20 - ___ = 16

505. 17 - ___ = 10

506. ___ - 3 = 8

507. ___ - 10 = 7

508. 5 - ___ = 1

509. 15 - 5 = ___

510. 14 - ___ = 6

511. 15 - 14 = ___

512. 17 - ___ = 14

513. 20 - ___ = 15

514. 12 - ___ = 6

515. 18 - 16 = ___

516. 6 - ___ = 0

517. 16 - 2 = ___

518. 20 - 19 = ___

519. ___ - 6 = 9

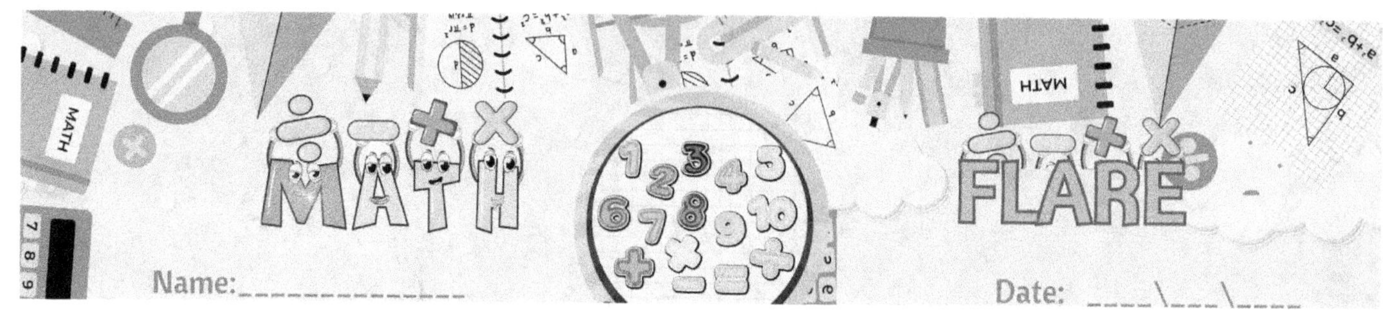

Subtraction 1 through 50

Find the Difference.

520.	521.	522.	523.	524.
17 − 7	15 − 11	14 − 12	11 − 11	20 − 16

525.	526.	527.	528.	529.
19 − 4	10 − 1	18 − 15	11 − 2	7 − 7

530.	531.	532.	533.	534.
10 − 7	7 − 1	11 − 9	17 − 10	2 − 1

535.	536.	537.	538.	539.
14 − 7	14 − 2	3 − 1	16 − 4	9 − 2

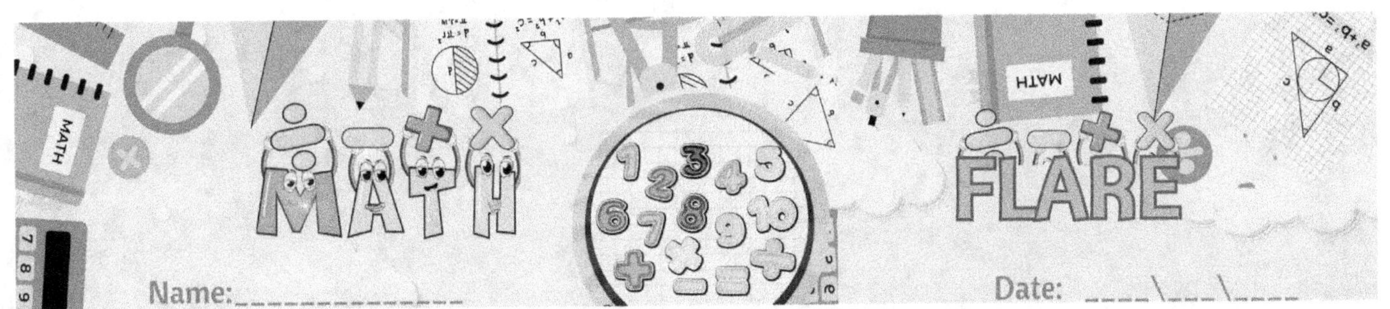

540. 16 − 7	541. 7 − 3	542. 15 − 15	543. 19 − 9	544. 1 − 1
545. 20 − 12	546. 15 − 3	547. 2 − 2	548. 4 − 4	549. 18 − 14
550. 4 − 3	551. 11 − 5	552. 19 − 15	553. 20 − 7	554. 5 − 1
555. 7 − 4	556. 12 − 8	557. 5 − 3	558. 10 − 2	559. 11 − 7
560. 4 − 2	561. 10 − 9	562. 10 − 8	563. 9 − 6	564. 17 − 1

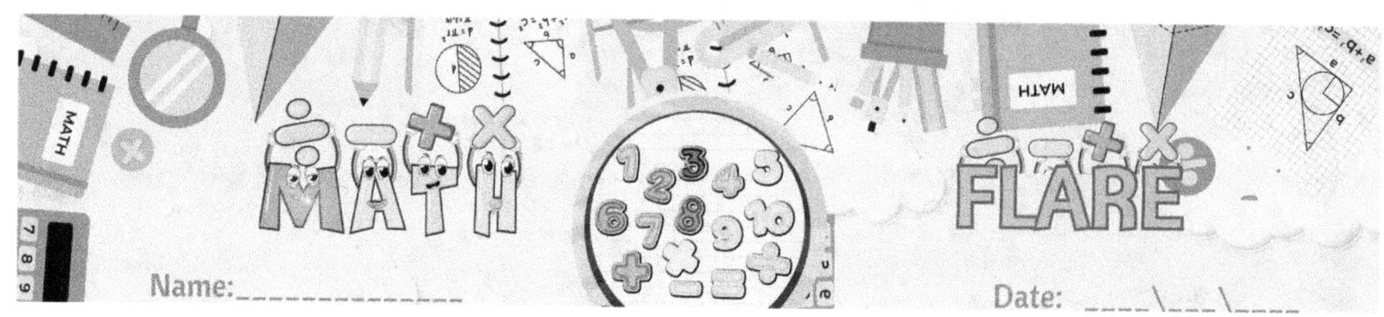

565. $\begin{array}{r} 7 \\ -\ 5 \\ \hline \end{array}$	566. $\begin{array}{r} 8 \\ -\ 3 \\ \hline \end{array}$	567. $\begin{array}{r} 3 \\ -\ 2 \\ \hline \end{array}$	568. $\begin{array}{r} 13 \\ -\ 11 \\ \hline \end{array}$	569. $\begin{array}{r} 5 \\ -\ 2 \\ \hline \end{array}$
570. $\begin{array}{r} 12 \\ -\ 10 \\ \hline \end{array}$	571. $\begin{array}{r} 18 \\ -\ 3 \\ \hline \end{array}$	572. $\begin{array}{r} 14 \\ -\ 6 \\ \hline \end{array}$	573. $\begin{array}{r} 14 \\ -\ 9 \\ \hline \end{array}$	574. $\begin{array}{r} 16 \\ -\ 8 \\ \hline \end{array}$
575. $\begin{array}{r} 5 \\ -\ 5 \\ \hline \end{array}$	576. $\begin{array}{r} 11 \\ -\ 3 \\ \hline \end{array}$	577. $\begin{array}{r} 20 \\ -\ 11 \\ \hline \end{array}$	578. $\begin{array}{r} 10 \\ -\ 4 \\ \hline \end{array}$	579. $\begin{array}{r} 16 \\ -\ 2 \\ \hline \end{array}$
580. $\begin{array}{r} 11 \\ -\ 8 \\ \hline \end{array}$	581. $\begin{array}{r} 12 \\ -\ 11 \\ \hline \end{array}$	582. $\begin{array}{r} 12 \\ -\ 6 \\ \hline \end{array}$	583. $\begin{array}{r} 18 \\ -\ 10 \\ \hline \end{array}$	584. $\begin{array}{r} 20 \\ -\ 3 \\ \hline \end{array}$
585. $\begin{array}{r} 16 \\ -\ 6 \\ \hline \end{array}$	586. $\begin{array}{r} 15 \\ -\ 9 \\ \hline \end{array}$	587. $\begin{array}{r} 17 \\ -\ 11 \\ \hline \end{array}$	588. $\begin{array}{r} 18 \\ -\ 12 \\ \hline \end{array}$	589. $\begin{array}{r} 8 \\ -\ 4 \\ \hline \end{array}$

590.	6	591.	12	592.	6	593.	12	594.	16
	− 1		− 9		− 5		− 2		− 9

595.	12	596.	7	597.	8	598.	17	599.	9
	− 4		− 6		− 6		− 5		− 4

600.	9	601.	10	602.	18	603.	13	604.	5
	− 3		− 6		− 2		− 6		− 4

605.	15	606.	9	607.	14	608.	16	609.	6
	− 6		− 5		− 3		− 10		− 2

610.	8	611.	6	612.	13	613.	13	614.	9
	− 5		− 3		− 9		− 7		− 7

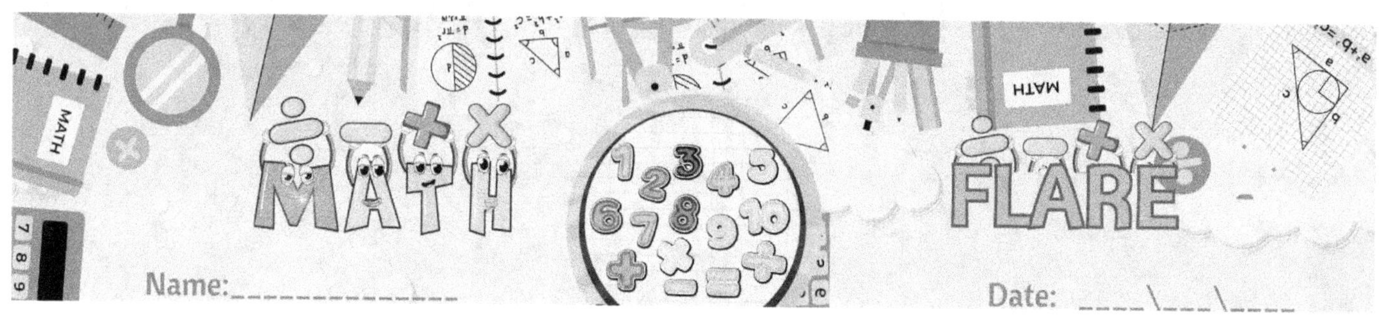

615. $\begin{array}{r} 20 \\ -\ 15 \\ \hline \end{array}$	616. $\begin{array}{r} 8 \\ -\ 7 \\ \hline \end{array}$	617. $\begin{array}{r} 18 \\ -\ 9 \\ \hline \end{array}$	618. $\begin{array}{r} 19 \\ -\ 13 \\ \hline \end{array}$	619. $\begin{array}{r} 13 \\ -\ 3 \\ \hline \end{array}$
620. $\begin{array}{r} 15 \\ -\ 12 \\ \hline \end{array}$	621. $\begin{array}{r} 19 \\ -\ 17 \\ \hline \end{array}$	622. $\begin{array}{r} 16 \\ -\ 13 \\ \hline \end{array}$	623. $\begin{array}{r} 18 \\ -\ 11 \\ \hline \end{array}$	624. $\begin{array}{r} 19 \\ -\ 18 \\ \hline \end{array}$
625. $\begin{array}{r} 9 \\ -\ 8 \\ \hline \end{array}$	626. $\begin{array}{r} 17 \\ -\ 6 \\ \hline \end{array}$	627. $\begin{array}{r} 7 \\ -\ 2 \\ \hline \end{array}$	628. $\begin{array}{r} 11 \\ -\ 1 \\ \hline \end{array}$	629. $\begin{array}{r} 11 \\ -\ 4 \\ \hline \end{array}$
630. $\begin{array}{r} 19 \\ -\ 5 \\ \hline \end{array}$	631. $\begin{array}{r} 15 \\ -\ 10 \\ \hline \end{array}$	632. $\begin{array}{r} 6 \\ -\ 6 \\ \hline \end{array}$	633. $\begin{array}{r} 8 \\ -\ 1 \\ \hline \end{array}$	634. $\begin{array}{r} 13 \\ -\ 2 \\ \hline \end{array}$
635. $\begin{array}{r} 17 \\ -\ 16 \\ \hline \end{array}$	636. $\begin{array}{r} 13 \\ -\ 4 \\ \hline \end{array}$	637. $\begin{array}{r} 6 \\ -\ 4 \\ \hline \end{array}$	638. $\begin{array}{r} 16 \\ -\ 3 \\ \hline \end{array}$	639. $\begin{array}{r} 11 \\ -\ 6 \\ \hline \end{array}$

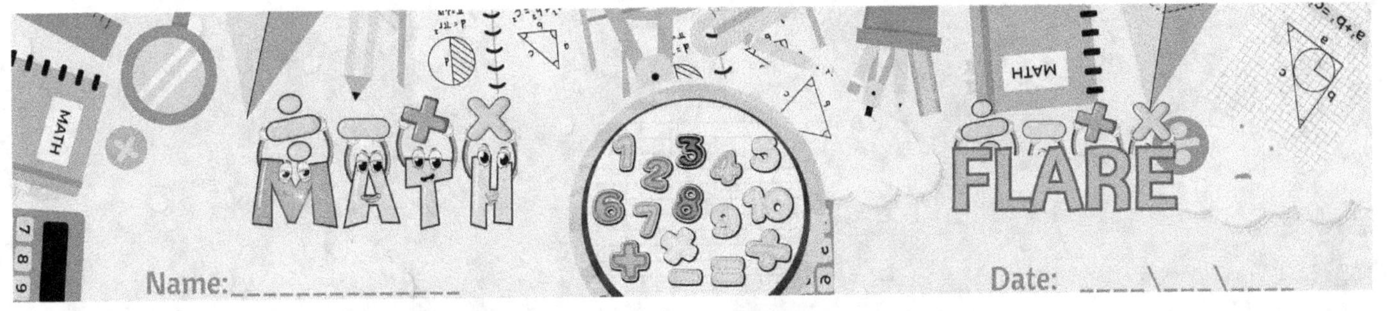

Name:_______________   Date: ___________

Commutative Property of Addition

Use the commutative property to fill the missing values.

640. $14 + 8 = \underline{} + 14$

641. $13 + 9 = 9 + \underline{}$

642. $17 + 8 = 8 + \underline{}$

643. $9 + \underline{} = 3 + 9$

644. $\underline{} + 11 = 11 + 4$

645. $14 + \underline{} = 10 + 14$

646. $6 + \underline{} = 9 + 6$

647. $\underline{} + 17 = 17 + 11$

648. $19 + 10 = 10 + \underline{}$

649. $3 + 4 = \underline{} + 3$

650. $14 + 19 = 19 + \underline{}$

651. $19 + 2 = \underline{} + 19$

652. $2 + 19 = \underline{} + 2$

653. $14 + 9 = 9 + \underline{}$

654. $20 + \underline{} = 15 + 20$

655. $9 + \underline{} = 5 + 9$

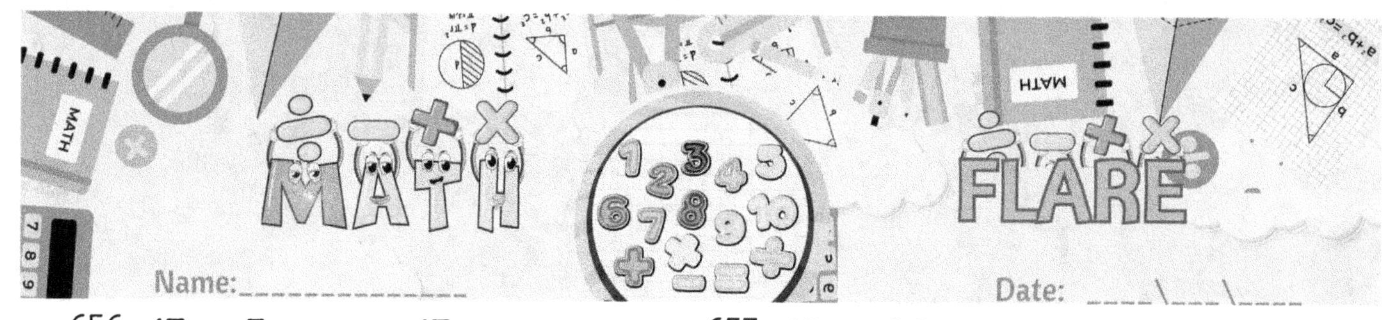

656. 17 + 3 = __ + 17

657. 18 + 20 = 20 + __

658. 3 + 11 = __ + 3

659. 19 + 18 = 18 + __

660. 9 + __ = 1 + 9

661. 20 + 8 = __ + 20

662. 3 + 9 = __ + 3

663. 4 + __ = 14 + 4

664. 10 + 1 = 1 + __

665. 3 + __ = 19 + 3

666. __ + 16 = 16 + 5

667. 18 + 15 = 15 + __

668. 10 + 12 = 12 + __

669. __ + 18 = 18 + 8

670. __ + 20 = 20 + 14

671. 3 + __ = 10 + 3

672. 13 + 5 = __ + 13

673. 12 + 11 = 11 + __

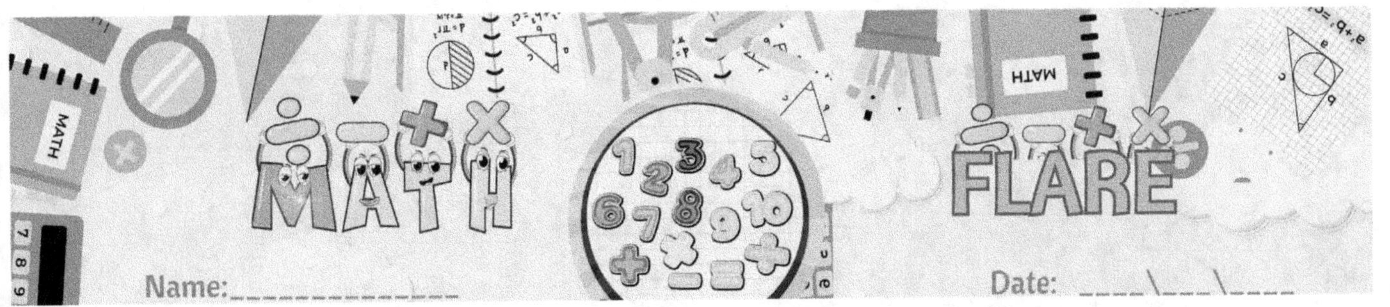

674. 16 + 8 = __ + 16

675. 11 + __ = 5 + 11

676. 15 + 13 = 13 + __

677. 20 + 11 = 11 + __

678. 19 + 13 = 13 + __

679. 16 + 19 = __ + 16

680. __ + 12 = 12 + 19

681. 10 + 2 = __ + 10

682. 2 + 5 = 5 + __

683. __ + 4 = 4 + 10

684. __ + 18 = 18 + 9

685. 11 + 6 = __ + 11

686. 12 + 16 = 16 + __

687. 19 + 4 = 4 + __

688. __ + 6 = 6 + 19

689. 15 + __ = 9 + 15

Name:________________ Date: _____________

Make 50

Find the unknow number to make 50.

690. 29 + ___ = 50

691. 36 + ___ = 50

692. 4 + ___ = 50

693. 33 + ___ = 50

694. 34 + ___ = 50

695. 13 + ___ = 50

696. 6 + ___ = 50

697. 30 + ___ = 50

698. 2 + ___ = 50

699. 3 + ___ = 50

700. 26 + ___ = 50

701. 15 + ___ = 50

702. 20 + ___ = 50

703. 23 + ___ = 50

704. 32 + ___ = 50

705. 9 + ___ = 50

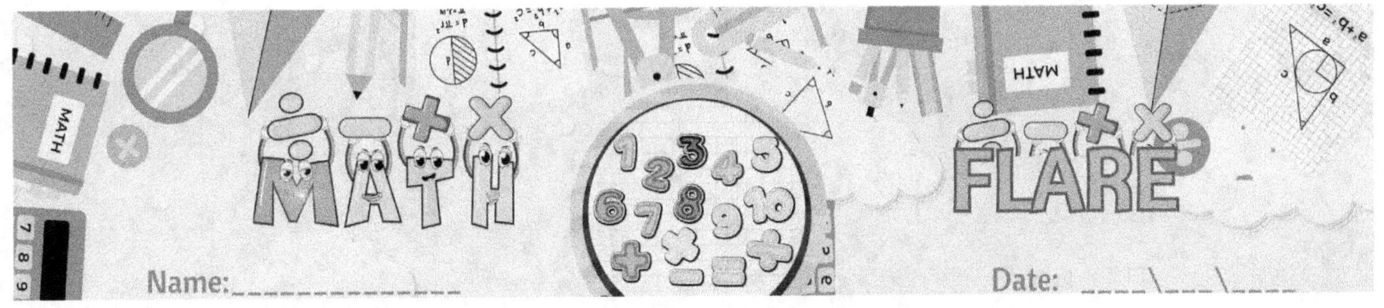

Name:_________________________   Date: _______________

706. 11 + ___ = 50

707. 31 + ___ = 50

708. 27 + ___ = 50

709. 10 + ___ = 50

710. 18 + ___ = 50

711. 5 + ___ = 50

712. 19 + ___ = 50

713. 7 + ___ = 50

714. 37 + ___ = 50

715. 16 + ___ = 50

716. 28 + ___ = 50

717. 14 + ___ = 50

718. 39 + ___ = 50

719. 17 + ___ = 50

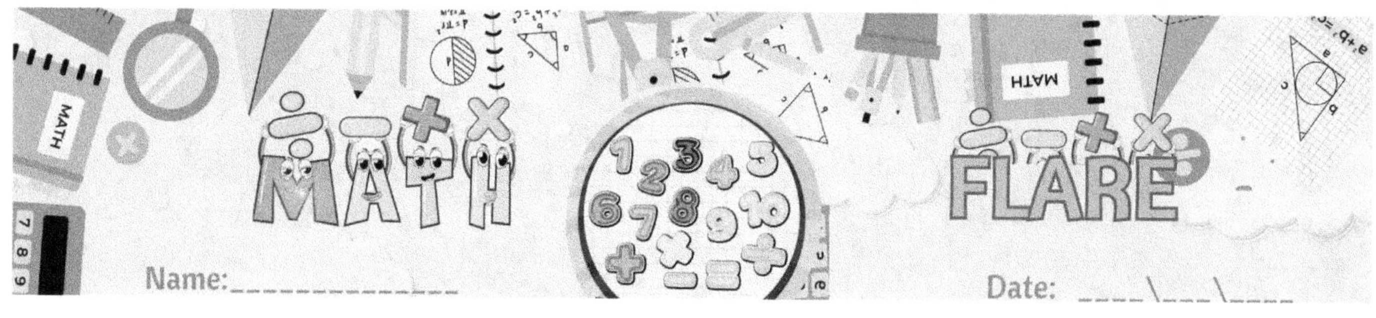

Matching the answers.

720.

a. 22 + 1 = _______ •	• B = 86
b. 23 + 20 = ______ •	• G = 10
c. 24 – 16 = ______ •	• H = 28
d. 13 – 3 = ______ •	• C = 23
e. 50 + 9 = ______ •	• J = 59
f. 7 – 1 = _______ •	• D = 4
g. 10 – 6 = ______ •	• F = 43
h. 48 + 38 = _____ •	• E = 6
i. 23 + 5 = ______ •	• I = 8
j. 45 + 40 = _____ •	• A = 85

721.

a. 39 - 32 = _______ •   • B = 3

b. 4 + 45 = _______ •   • G = 6

c. 45 - 37 = _______ •   • C = 67

d. 16 - 6 = _______ •   • I = 10

e. 24 - 3 = _______ •   • J = 21

f. 38 - 35 = _______ •   • H = 54

g. 43 + 11 = _______ •   • A = 49

h. 39 - 33 = _______ •   • F = 7

i. 32 + 35 = _______ •   • E = 8

j. 37 - 15 = _______ •   • D = 22

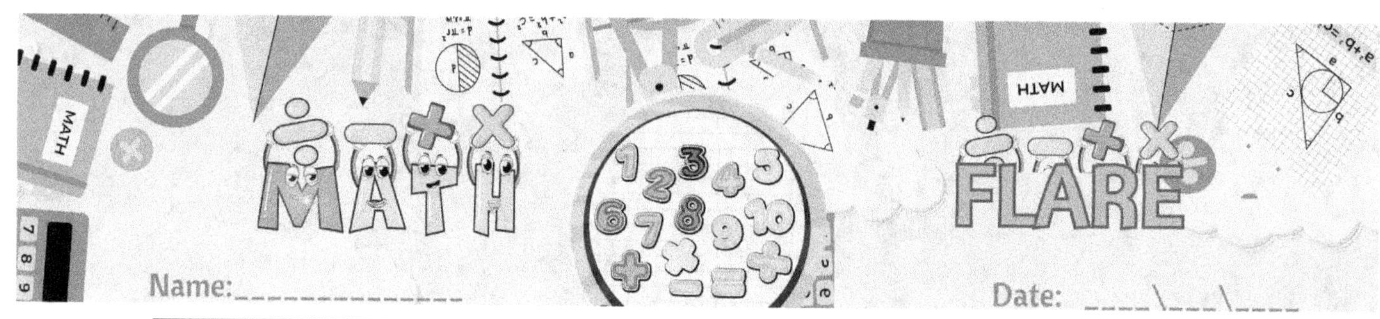

722.

a. 47 - 38 = _______ •

b. 34 + 38 = _______ •

c. 21 - 7 = _______ •

d. 32 - 22 = _______ •

e. 15 - 3 = _______ •

f. 3 + 36 = _______ •

g. 47 - 16 = _______ •

h. 34 + 7 = _______ •

i. 50 + 5 = _______ •

j. 35 - 16 = _______ •

• F = 9

• E = 10

• B = 14

• J = 39

• G = 72

• I = 31

• A = 41

• H = 19

• D = 12

• C = 55

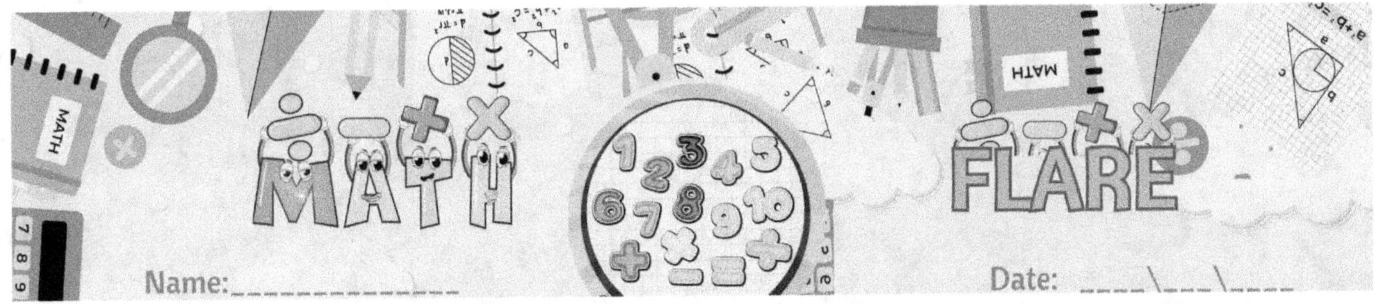

723.

a. 19 - 16 = _______   •

b. 5 + 6 = _______   •

c. 15 + 19 = _______   •

d. 34 - 8 = _______   •

e. 49 + 18 = _______   •

f. 18 + 33 = _______   •

g. 38 + 18 = _______   •

h. 35 - 4 = _______   •

i. 28 + 38 = _______   •

j. 38 - 6 = _______   •

• F = 51

• C = 67

• I = 11

• E = 26

• J = 66

• D = 32

• B = 31

• A = 34

• G = 56

• H = 3

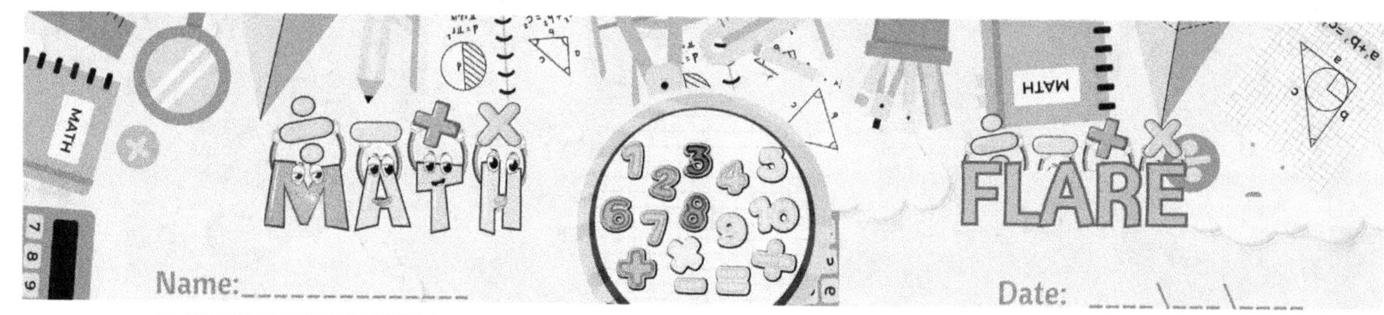

724.

a. 48 − 13 = ______ •	• E = 9
b. 19 − 1 = ______ •	• C = 35
c. 40 − 1 = ______ •	• A = 12
d. 19 − 17 = ______ •	• B = 20
e. 27 − 15 = ______ •	• G = 2
f. 9 + 13 = ______ •	• H = 46
g. 28 + 18 = ______ •	• F = 39
h. 27 + 13 = ______ •	• I = 18
i. 36 − 27 = ______ •	• D = 22
j. 47 − 27 = ______ •	• J = 40

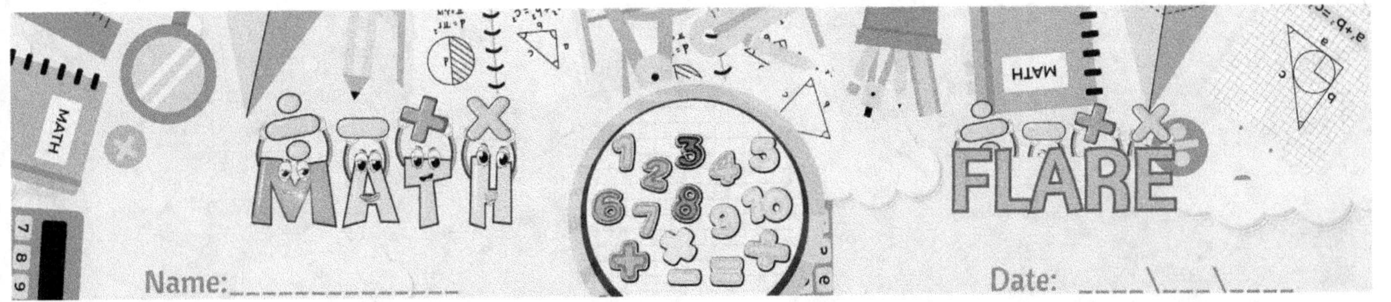

725.

a. 35 + 25 = _______ •	• C = 5
b. 35 - 30 = _______ •	• G = 5
c. 4 + 10 = _______ •	• B = 60
d. 38 - 20 = _______ •	• D = 35
e. 9 - 7 = _______ •	• I = 40
f. 32 - 15 = _______ •	• H = 2
g. 14 + 21 = _______ •	• J = 18
h. 43 - 3 = _______ •	• E = 14
i. 30 - 25 = _______ •	• A = 1
j. 9 - 8 = _______ •	• F = 17

726.

a. 36 + 15 = _______ •

b. 50 + 17 = _______ •

c. 2 - 2 = _______ •

d. 22 - 21 = _______ •

e. 16 - 14 = _______ •

f. 30 + 31 = _______ •

g. 46 + 26 = _______ •

h. 28 + 23 = _______ •

i. 42 - 33 = _______ •

j. 1 - 1 = _______ •

• I = 0

• H = 72

• J = 67

• G = 51

• A = 51

• C = 1

• D = 0

• F = 61

• E = 9

• B = 2

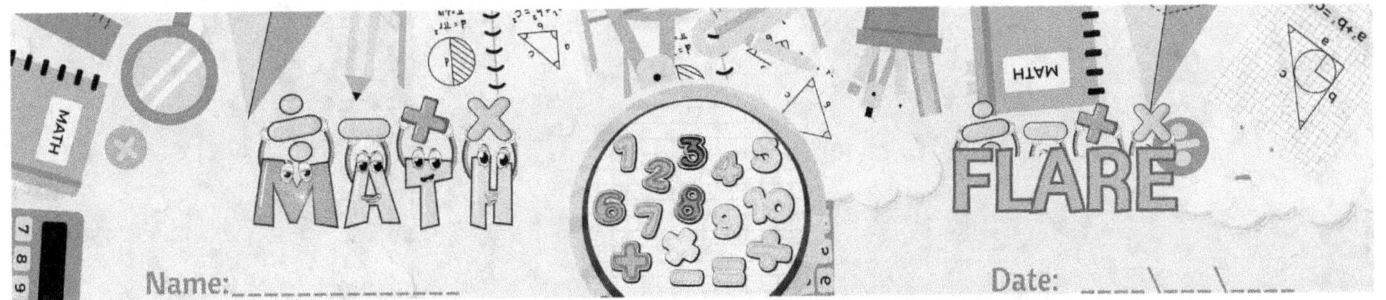

727.

a. 35 + 2 = _______ •	• C = 64
b. 36 + 21 = _______ •	• F = 57
c. 7 - 2 = _______ •	• I = 20
d. 20 + 10 = _______ •	• H = 37
e. 31 + 27 = _______ •	• J = 5
f. 23 - 3 = _______ •	• B = 30
g. 50 + 14 = _______ •	• G = 34
h. 35 - 1 = _______ •	• D = 52
i. 13 - 6 = _______ •	• E = 7
j. 42 + 10 = _______ •	• A = 58

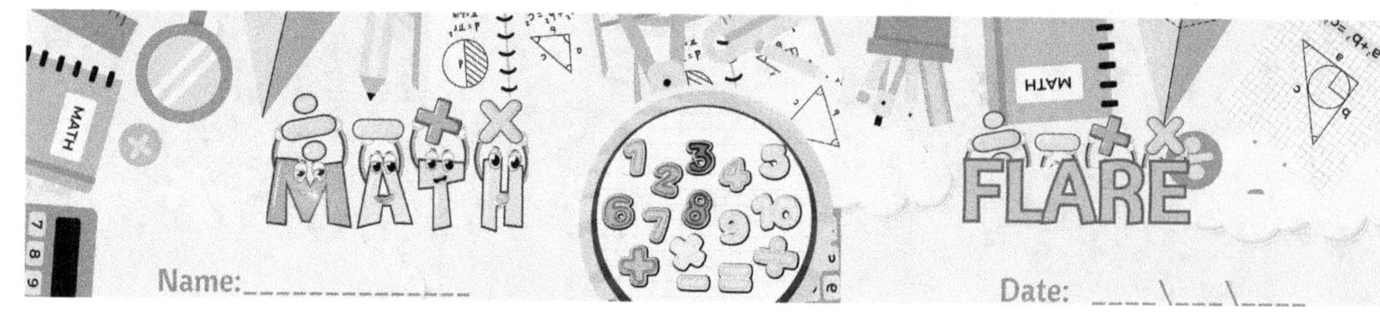

728.

a. 26 − 4 = _______ •	• E = 5
b. 9 − 9 = _______ •	• F = 37
c. 26 − 20 = _____ •	• A = 68
d. 48 − 11 = _____ •	• I = 6
e. 27 − 22 = _____ •	• J = 3
f. 28 + 40 = _____ •	• G = 14
g. 42 + 12 = _____ •	• B = 22
h. 21 + 16 = _____ •	• C = 0
i. 5 − 2 = _______ •	• H = 54
j. 17 − 3 = _______ •	• D = 37

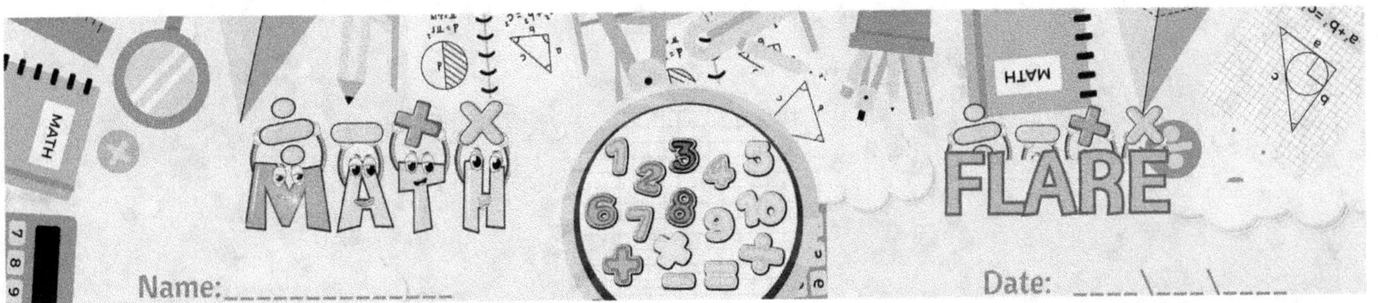

729.

a. 8 – 3 = _______ •	• G = 12
b. 28 – 16 = _______ •	• I = 57
c. 40 + 21 = _______ •	• B = 58
d. 18 – 13 = _______ •	• E = 59
e. 47 + 11 = _______ •	• C = 5
f. 32 + 5 = _______ •	• H = 5
g. 37 – 17 = _______ •	• D = 37
h. 40 – 12 = _______ •	• A = 28
i. 30 + 27 = _______ •	• F = 61
j. 33 + 26 = _______ •	• J = 20

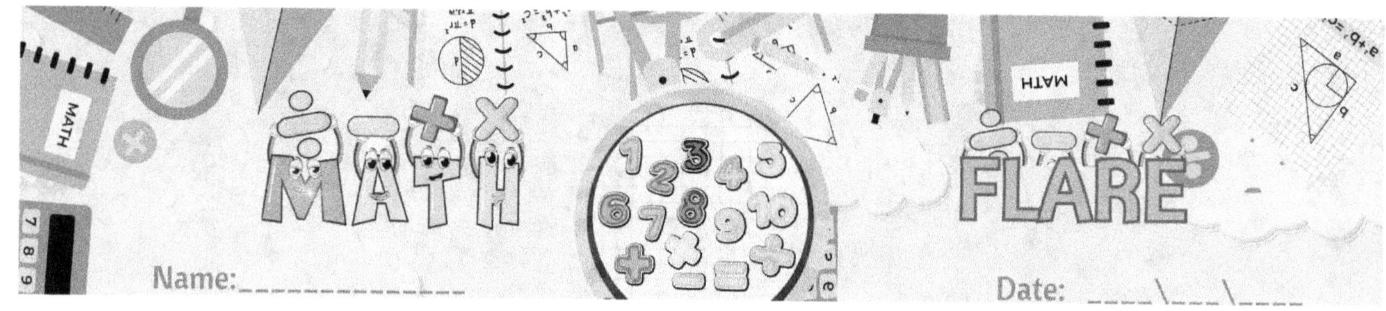

Addition Word Problems

730. Ariana has 8 trees. Her friend gives her 4 more trees. How many trees does Ariana have now?

731. A machine has 2 parts. If 7 more parts are added, how many parts does the machine have now?

732. Lila has 1 bat in a bag. If Lila adds 5 more bats to the bag, how many bats does Lila have in total?

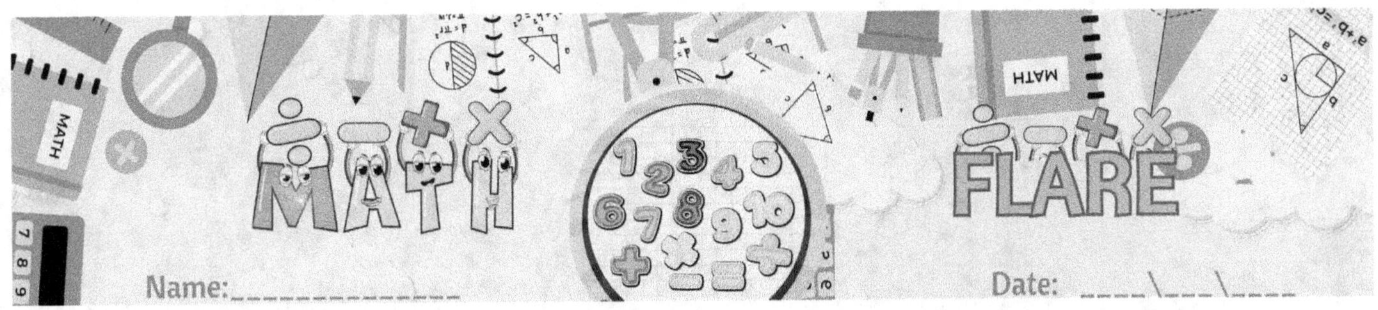

733. A basketball team scored 1 points in the first quarter and 7 points in the second quarter. What was the total score of the basketball team after the first half?

734. Christian had 1 dollars in the morning and earned 1 more dollars in the afternoon. How many dollars Christian have in total?

735. At the start of the week, 2 chocolates were in the store. By the end of the week, 7 more chocolates were added to the store. How many chocolates are in the store now?

736. Brandon has 10 towels and buys 7 more towels. How many towels does Brandon have in total?

737. Dominic has 3 pencils and 6 pens. If Dominic puts all the writing utensils in a case, how many writing utensils are in the case in total?

738. The weight of an empty container is 2 pounds. If the container is filled with 9 pounds of toothpastes, what is the total weight of the container and its contents?

739. A basket holds 3 scarves. If 5 more scarves are added to the basket, how many scarves will the basket hold in total?

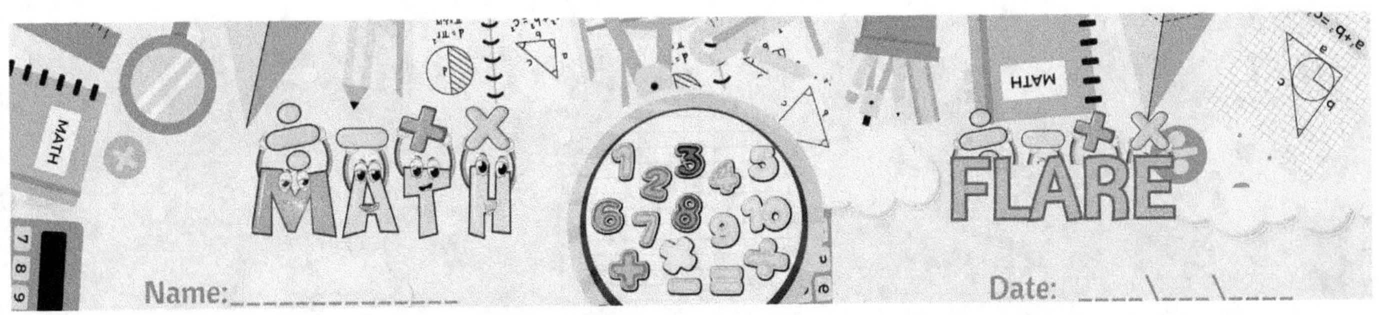

740. An object has 5 parts. If 6 more parts are added, how many parts does the object have now?

741. There are 6 crows on a tree. 10 more crows land on the tree. How many crows are on the tree now?

742. Carter drove 10 miles in the morning and 1 miles in the evening. How many miles did Carter drive in total?

743. Hunter has a basket with 4 erasers in it. After buying 3 more erasers, how many erasers does Hunter have in total?

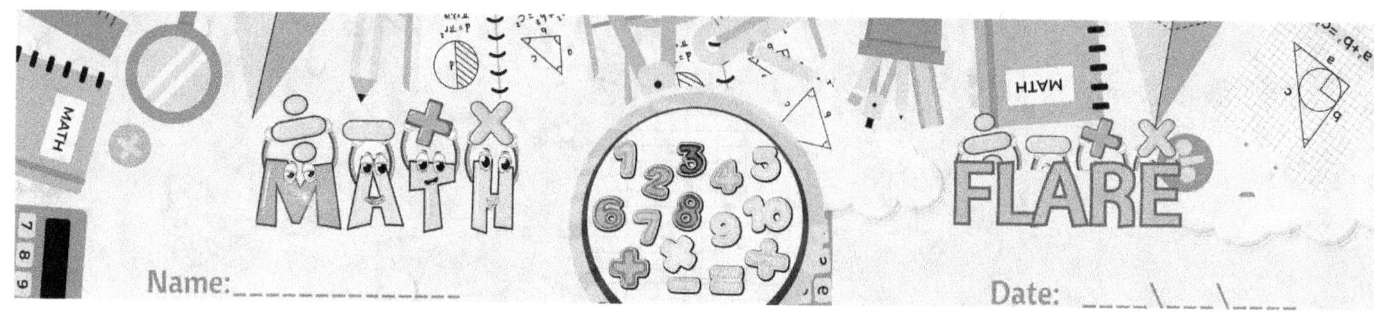

744. A bus made 7 stops in the morning and 5 stops in the afternoon. How many stops did the bus make in total?

745. Alexander has 8 thermometers. He finds 4 more thermometers. How many thermometers does he have now?

746. On Monday, Maya caught 4 fish, and on Tuesday, Maya caught 10 fish. How many fish did Maya catch in total?

747. There are 7 kids playing on the playground. 1 more kids join them. How many kids are playing now?

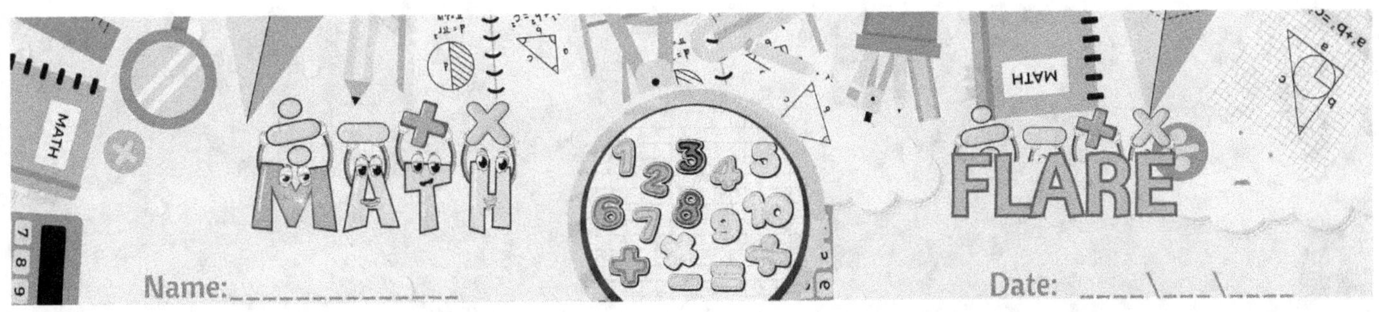

748. Diego filled a tank with 7 gallons of gas and then added 6 more gallons. How many gallons of gas are in the tank now?

749. There were 1 people in line at the store. After 4 more people joined the line, how many people are in the line now?

750. There is 1 trees in the garden. 6 more trees are planted. How many trees are in the garden now?

751. Arianna bought 10 pencils and later bought 4 pencils. How many pencils does Arianna have now?

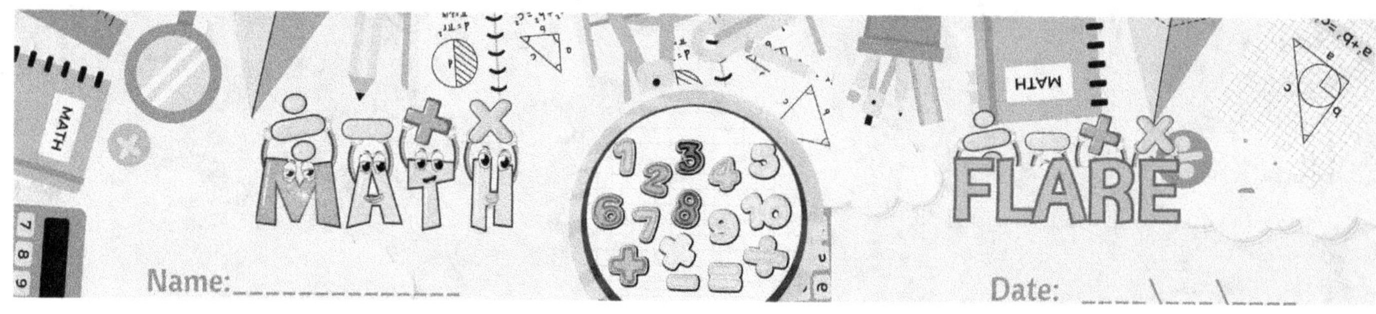

752. Leo has 3 gloves. He receives 6 more gloves. How many gloves does he have now?

753. There are 3 gauzes in the room. 8 more gauzes are brought in. How many gauzes are in the room now?

754. Abigail wrote 2 pages of her book yesterday and 2 pages today. How many pages did she write in total?

755. Dylan made 3 cookies and Maria made 2 cookies. How many cookies were made in total?

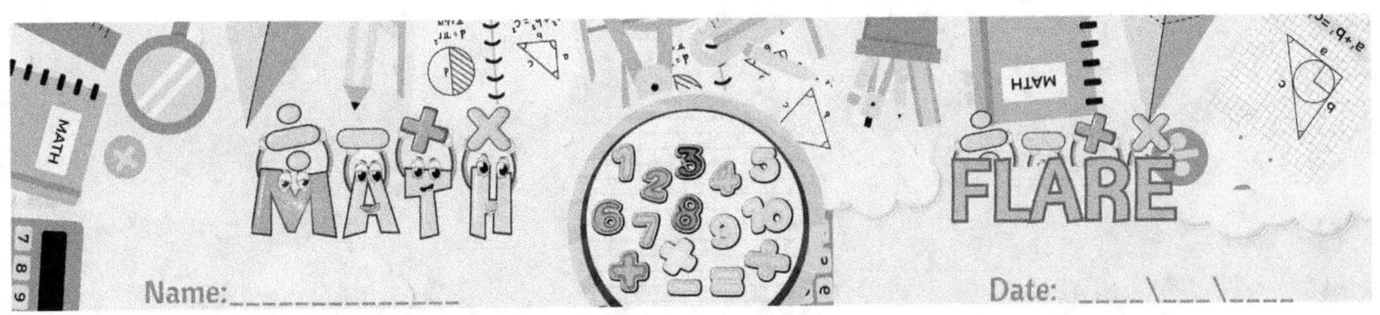

756. Serenity baked 1 cakes yesterday and 2 cakes today. How many cakes did Serenity bake in total?

757. Owen has 10 fish in an aquarium. If Owen adds 2 more fish to the aquarium, how many fish will be in the aquarium in total?

758. Ethan has 8 red compasses and 2 green compasses. If Ethan puts all the compasses in a basket, how many compasses are in the basket in total?

759. Aurora has 8 radios. She buys 10 more radios at the store. How many radios does Aurora have now?

Subtraction Word Problems

760. A cake recipe calls for 9 cups of flour. 4 cups of flour have already been added. How many more cups of flour are needed?

761. There is 1 cars in a parking lot. Roman took 1 cars out of the lot. How many cars are still in the lot?

762. Lincoln had 8 carrots. He gave 2 carrots to Hazel. How many carrots does Lincoln have left?

763. There are 4 turtles in a pond. If 4 leave, how many turtles are left in the pond?

764. Easton has 1 dollars. He needs to buy bananas that costs 3 dollars. How much money will he have left after buying the bananas?

765. A box of calculators weighs 5 pounds. If you remove 3 pounds from it, how much does it weigh now?

766. Everleigh has 1 dollars. She wants to buy hats, which costs 1 dollars. How much more money does she need to buy it?

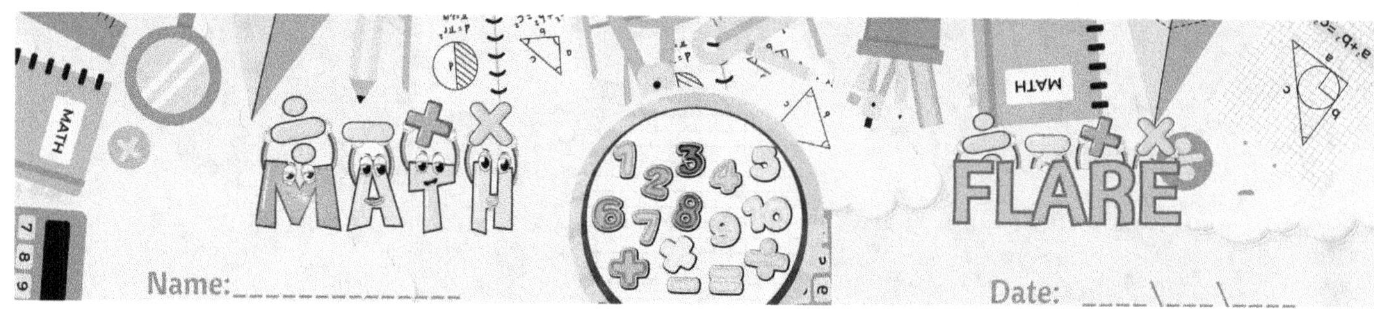

767. Aaliyah baked a 1 cookies. 1 of them were chocolate chip cookies and the rest were oatmeal raisin cookies. How many oatmeal raisin cookies did Aaliyah bake?

768. Aurora and Alice went shopping for desks. They had 7 dollars to spend but 4 dollars ended up being spent. How much money do they have left?

769. Paisley and Lydia went on a shopping spree and bought 4 shirts. After returning home, they realized that they didn't need 1 of them. How many shirts did they end up keeping?

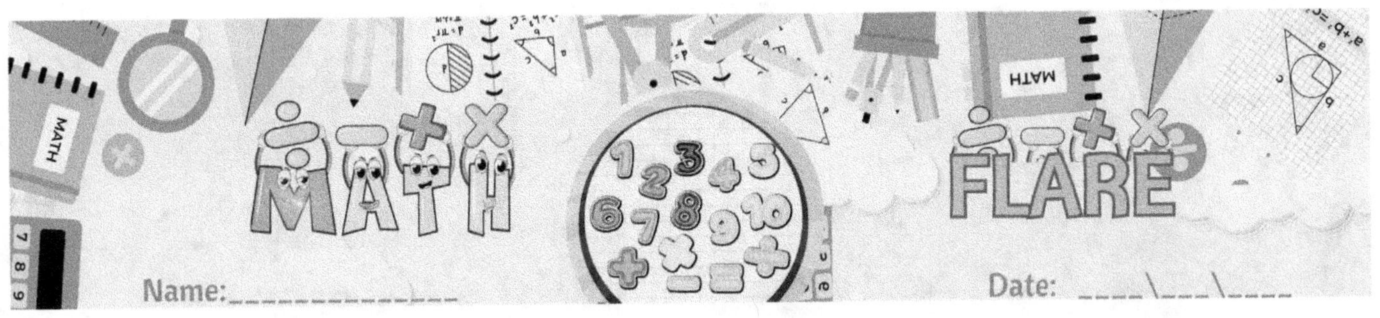

770. A pizza has 1 slices. Reagan ate 1 slices. How many slices of pizza are left?

771. There were 2 students in a class. 1 of them were absent. How many students were present in the class?

772. There are 6 dogs in a park. If 1 leave, how many dogs are left in the park?

773. Alexa wants to buy combs, which costs 10 dollars. She has 10 dollars and plans to save the rest. How much more money does she need to save to buy combs?

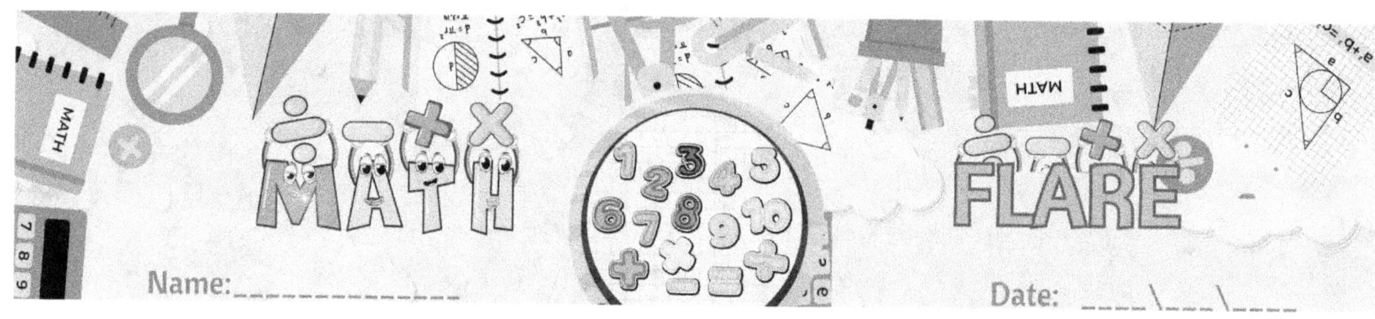

774. A pack of gum had 9 pieces. Mia took 7 pieces of gum. How many pieces of gum are left in the pack?

775. Zoey has 7 towels. She lost 2 of them. How many towels does Zoey have left?

776. Arianna bought gloves for 6 dollars. She received 5 dollars in change. How much did gloves cost?

777. If you have 5 shoes and you give away 3, how many shoes do you have left?

778. Naomi bought radios for 7 dollars but later found out it was on sale for 7 dollars less. How much did she overpay for radios?

779. A recipe needs 9 cups of sugar. Mila added 2 cups of sugar. How many cups of sugar are still needed?

780. Isaac has 8 red coins and 2 green coins. How many more red coins does Isaac have than green coins?

781. Gemma has 1 gloves. She gave 1 gloves to Lila. How many gloves does Gemma have now?

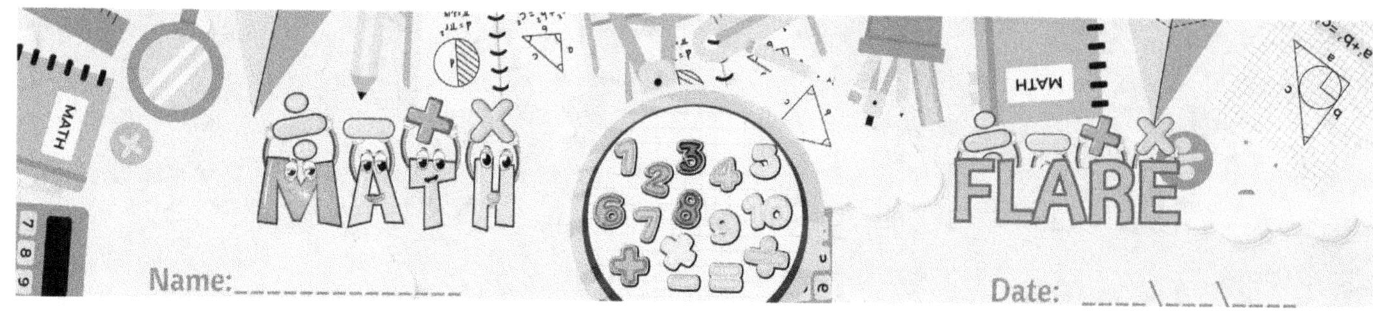

782. Justin saved up 7 dollars to buy bags. He spent 5 dollars on it. How much money does he have left?

783. Owen is 7 years old and Dominic is 1 years old. What is the difference in their ages?

784. There are 4 pants. 3 pants are blue and the rest are red. How many red pants are in the box?

785. A box had 6 chocolates. Scarlett ate 5 chocolates. How many chocolates are left in the box?

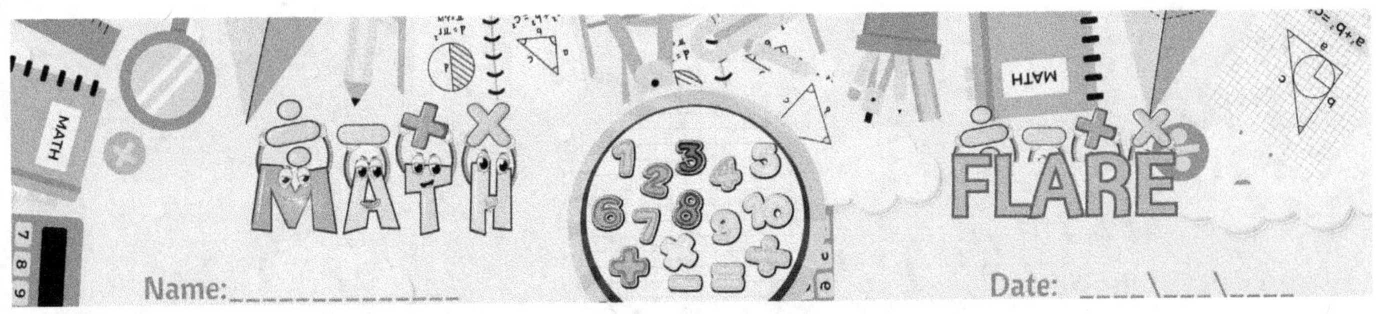

786. Bella bought forks for 8 dollars. She later returned some forks and received a refund of 3 dollars. How much money did she end up spending on forks?

787. Raelynn had 4 dollars. She spent 3 dollars on surgical masks. How much money does Raelynn have left?

788. Ryan has 5 shampoos. He traded 5 of them with his friend. How many shampoos does Ryan have now?

789. Toothbrushes originally cost 7 dollars, but it is now on sale for 6 dollars. How much money can you save by buying it on sale?

ANSWERS

Page 1: Addition 1 through 20

1. 22	2. 27	3. 22	4. 18	5. 13	6. 19	7. 19	8. 35
9. 28	10. 26	11. 19	12. 23	13. 18	14. 30	15. 7	16. 27
17. 22	18. 27	19. 27	20. 25	21. 8	22. 20	23. 28	24. 25
25. 34	26. 14	27. 11	28. 20	29. 16	30. 19	31. 21	32. 19
33. 28	34. 14	35. 20	36. 20	37. 17	38. 7	39. 29	40. 22
41. 14	42. 22	43. 19	44. 20	45. 17	46. 19	47. 35	48. 25
49. 12	50. 32	51. 26	52. 15	53. 16	54. 20	55. 15	56. 21
57. 23	58. 10	59. 27	60. 27	61. 20	62. 23	63. 14	64. 16
65. 22	66. 21	67. 33	68. 9	69. 26	70. 29	71. 24	72. 25
73. 18	74. 29	75. 25	76. 20	77. 34	78. 31	79. 17	80. 25
81. 7	82. 25	83. 23	84. 5	85. 16	86. 36	87. 14	88. 15
89. 8	90. 13	91. 6	92. 14	93. 21	94. 18	95. 37	96. 14
97. 20	98. 7	99. 29	100. 22				

Page 5: Addition 1 through 20

101. 11	102. 17	103. 15	104. 20	105. 18	106. 15	107. 25
108. 15	109. 33	110. 16	111. 28	112. 17	113. 17	114. 1
115. 38	116. 5	117. 17	118. 14	119. 13	120. 20	121. 12
122. 6	123. 5	124. 18	125. 17	126. 14	127. 9	128. 20
129. 10	130. 12	131. 8	132. 11	133. 16	134. 3	135. 31

136. 9	137. 19	138. 30	139. 16	140. 10	141. 7	142. 19
143. 8	144. 28	145. 4	146. 7	147. 10	148. 15	149. 2
150. 7	151. 11	152. 14	153. 6	154. 9	155. 26	156. 21
157. 5	158. 7	159. 7	160. 2	161. 24	162. 10	163. 27
164. 10	165. 9	166. 6	167. 18	168. 2	169. 2	170. 14
171. 22	172. 13	173. 1	174. 16	175. 5	176. 14	177. 5
178. 19	179. 18	180. 5	181. 14	182. 29	183. 13	184. 14
185. 3	186. 16	187. 15	188. 4	189. 15	190. 16	191. 10
192. 9	193. 11	194. 15	195. 20	196. 6	197. 16	198. 12

Page 10: Addition 1 through 50

199. 30	200. 19	201. 13	202. 36	203. 56	204. 65	205. 50
206. 53	207. 63	208. 20	209. 21	210. 39	211. 34	212. 47
213. 16	214. 31	215. 26	216. 68	217. 16	218. 51	219. 61
220. 41	221. 24	222. 75	223. 60	224. 49	225. 42	226. 60
227. 91	228. 89	229. 77	230. 26	231. 41	232. 35	233. 16
234. 72	235. 27	236. 57	237. 59	238. 50	239. 64	240. 63
241. 44	242. 25	243. 72	244. 22	245. 10	246. 29	247. 62
248. 29	249. 26	250. 58	251. 60	252. 44	253. 27	254. 25
255. 96	256. 59	257. 50	258. 25	259. 28	260. 48	261. 21
262. 57	263. 39	264. 25	265. 44	266. 51	267. 18	268. 73
269. 20	270. 66	271. 63	272. 26	273. 69	274. 51	275. 50

276. 47   277. 61   278. 50   279. 30   280. 87   281. 52   282. 28

283. 66   284. 37   285. 21   286. 60   287. 27   288. 67   289. 79

290. 79   291. 58   292. 37   293. 33   294. 48   295. 94   296. 31

297. 61   298. 46   299. 74   300. 29   301. 40   302. 50   303. 90

304. 58   305. 64   306. 79   307. 66   308. 62   309. 56   310. 87

311. 55   312. 14   313. 86   314. 68   315. 56   316. 47   317. 36

318. 76

Page 15: Subtraction 1 through 20

319. 1   320. 1   321. 0   322. 5   323. 8   324. 8   325. 5   326. 2

327. 5   328. 14   329. 1   330. 3   331. 10   332. 10   333. 4   334. 1

335. 0   336. 5   337. 1   338. 2   339. 1   340. 0   341. 14   342. 4

343. 2   344. 0   345. 2   346. 3   347. 11   348. 3   349. 3   350. 3

351. 4   352. 16   353. 5   354. 5   355. 5   356. 6   357. 9   358. 13

359. 6   360. 13   361. 1   362. 2   363. 0   364. 2   365. 1   366. 2

367. 14   368. 2   369. 9   370. 13   371. 1   372. 0   373. 3   374. 16

375. 3   376. 10   377. 4   378. 0   379. 3   380. 11   381. 10   382. 1

383. 12   384. 7   385. 3   386. 3   387. 7   388. 6   389. 9   390. 5

391. 2   392. 11   393. 6   394. 0   395. 1   396. 2   397. 4   398. 8

399. 1   400. 7   401. 7   402. 4   403. 12   404. 11   405. 0   406. 2

407. 6   408. 12   409. 3   410. 5   411. 5   412. 4   413. 4

Page 19: Subtraction 1 through 20

414. 8	415. 7	416. 3	417. 7	418. 2	419. 5	420. 8
421. 11	422. 9	423. 1	424. 7	425. 3	426. 4	427. 5
428. 1	429. 5	430. 2	431. 11	432. 15	433. 10	434. 18
435. 7	436. 4	437. 9	438. 16	439. 2	440. 7	441. 19
442. 11	443. 4	444. 17	445. 16	446. 2	447. 12	448. 14
449. 2	450. 7	451. 10	452. 1	453. 2	454. 4	455. 5
456. 2	457. 1	458. 12	459. 0	460. 3	461. 7	462. 6
463. 6	464. 16	465. 4	466. 6	467. 6	468. 2	469. 4
470. 10	471. 12	472. 9	473. 2	474. 17	475. 11	476. 3
477. 1	478. 14	479. 8	480. 9	481. 13	482. 2	483. 2
484. 3	485. 7	486. 7	487. 15	488. 8	489. 2	490. 10
491. 12	492. 3	493. 17	494. 11	495. 6	496. 1	497. 2
498. 1	499. 4	500. 16	501. 12	502. 5	503. 7	504. 4
505. 7	506. 11	507. 17	508. 4	509. 10	510. 8	511. 1
512. 3	513. 5	514. 6	515. 2	516. 6	517. 14	518. 1
519. 15						

Page 25: Subtraction 1 through 50

520. 10	521. 4	522. 2	523. 0	524. 4	525. 15	526. 9	527. 3
528. 9	529. 0	530. 3	531. 6	532. 2	533. 7	534. 1	535. 7
536. 12	537. 2	538. 12	539. 7	540. 9	541. 4	542. 0	543. 10

544. 0 545. 8 546. 12 547. 0 548. 0 549. 4 550. 1 551. 6

552. 4 553. 13 554. 4 555. 3 556. 4 557. 2 558. 8 559. 4

560. 2 561. 1 562. 2 563. 3 564. 16 565. 2 566. 5 567. 1

568. 2 569. 3 570. 2 571. 15 572. 8 573. 5 574. 8 575. 0

576. 8 577. 9 578. 6 579. 14 580. 3 581. 1 582. 6 583. 8

584. 17 585. 10 586. 6 587. 6 588. 6 589. 4 590. 5 591. 3

592. 1 593. 10 594. 7 595. 8 596. 1 597. 2 598. 12 599. 5

600. 6 601. 4 602. 16 603. 7 604. 1 605. 9 606. 4 607. 11

608. 6 609. 4 610. 3 611. 3 612. 4 613. 6 614. 2 615. 5

616. 1 617. 9 618. 6 619. 10 620. 3 621. 2 622. 3 623. 7

624. 1 625. 1 626. 11 627. 5 628. 10 629. 7 630. 14 631. 5

632. 0 633. 7 634. 11 635. 1 636. 9 637. 2 638. 13 639. 5

Page 30: Commutative Property of Addition

640. 8 641. 13 642. 17 643. 3 644. 4 645. 10 646. 9 647. 11

648. 19 649. 4 650. 14 651. 2 652. 19 653. 14 654. 15 655. 5

656. 3 657. 18 658. 11 659. 19 660. 1 661. 8 662. 9 663. 14

664. 10 665. 19 666. 5 667. 18 668. 10 669. 8 670. 14 671. 10

672. 5 673. 12 674. 8 675. 5 676. 15 677. 20 678. 19 679. 19

680. 19 681. 2 682. 2 683. 10 684. 9 685. 6 686. 12 687. 19

688. 19 689. 9

Page 33: Make 50

690. 21	691. 14	692. 46	693. 17	694. 16	695. 37	696. 44
697. 20	698. 48	699. 47	700. 24	701. 35	702. 30	703. 27
704. 18	705. 41	706. 39	707. 19	708. 23	709. 40	710. 32
711. 45	712. 31	713. 43	714. 13	715. 34	716. 22	717. 36
718. 11	719. 33					

Page 35: Matching the answers.

720. a.C b.F c.I d.G e.J f.E g.D h.B i.H j.A

721. a.F b.A c.E d.I e.J f.B g.H h.G i.C j.D

722. a.F b.G c.B d.E e.D f.J g.I h.A i.C j.H

723. a.H b.I c.A d.E e.C f.F g.G h.B i.J j.D

724. a.C b.I c.F d.G e.A f.D g.H h.J i.E j.B

725. a.B b.G c.E d.J e.H f.F g.D h.I i.C j.A

726. a.A b.J c.D d.C e.B f.F g.H h.G i.E j.I

727. a.H b.F c.J d.B e.A f.I g.C h.G i.E j.D

728. a.B b.C c.I d.D e.E f.A g.H h.F i.J j.G

729. a.C b.G c.F d.H e.B f.D g.J h.A i.I j.E

Page 45: Addition Word Problems

730. 12	731. 9	732. 6	733. 8	734. 2	735. 9	736. 17	737. 9
738. 11	739. 8	740. 11	741. 16	742. 11	743. 7	744. 12	745. 12
746. 14	747. 8	748. 13	749. 5	750. 7	751. 14	752. 9	753. 11

754. 4   755. 5   756. 3   757. 12   758. 10   759. 18

Page 53: Subtraction Word Problems

760. 5   761. 0   762. 6   763. 0   764. 2   765. 2   766. 0   767. 0   768. 3

769. 3   770. 0   771. 1   772. 5   773. 0   774. 2   775. 5   776. 1   777. 2

778. 0   779. 7   780. 6   781. 0   782. 2   783. 6   784. 1   785. 1   786. 5

787. 1   788. 0   789. 1

MathFlare
Counting
and
Numbers
MATH WORKBOOK
Grade 1
Step by Step Guide and Essential Practice with Answers
Skip Counting
Count up and Down
Count by 2s and 3s
Number Sense

MathFlare
Addition
and
Subtraction
MATH WORKBOOK
Grade 1
Step by Step Guide and Essential Practice with Answers
Addition
Subtraction
Word Problems
Fact Families

MathFlare
Place Value
and
Expanded Notations
MATH WORKBOOK
Grade 1
Step by Step Guide and Essential Practice with Answers
Place Value
Expanded Notation
Words to Standard
Standard to Words

MathFlare
Addition
and
Subtraction
MATH WORKBOOK
Grade 1-2
Step by Step Guide and Essential Practice with Answers
Addition
Subtraction
Word Problems
Commutative Property

MathFlare
Counting
and
Numbers
MATH WORKBOOK
Grade 1-2
Step by Step Guide and Essential Practice with Answers
Count up and Down
Counting Patterns
Number Sense
Ordering Numbers

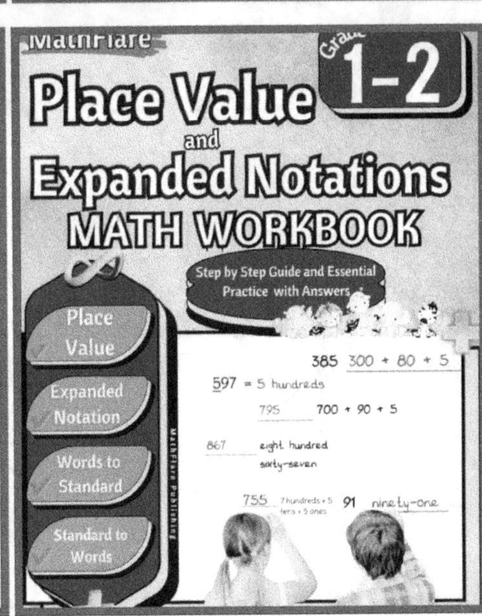

MathFlare
Place Value
and
Expanded Notations
MATH WORKBOOK
Grade 1-2
Step by Step Guide and Essential Practice with Answers
Place Value
Expanded Notation
Words to Standard
Standard to Words

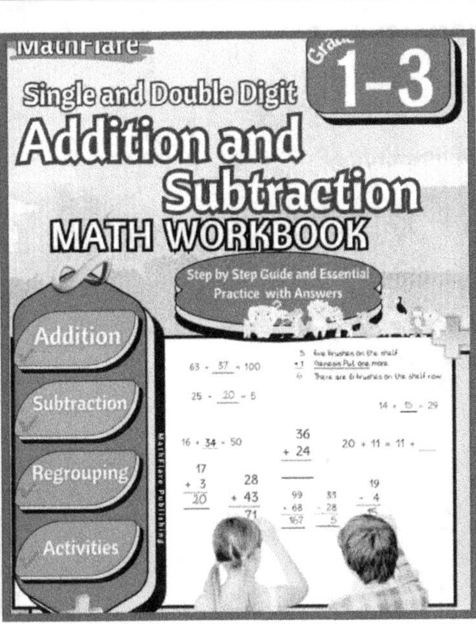

MathFlare
Single and Double Digit
Addition and
Subtraction
MATH WORKBOOK
Grade 1-3
Step by Step Guide and Essential Practice with Answers
Addition
Subtraction
Regrouping
Activities

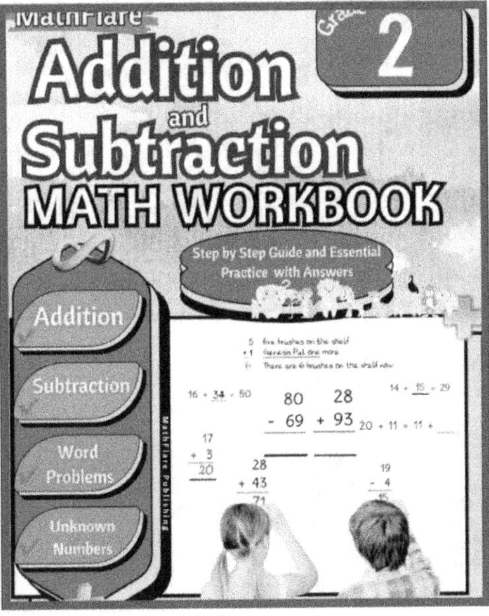

MathFlare
Addition
and
Subtraction
MATH WORKBOOK
Grade 2
Step by Step Guide and Essential Practice with Answers
Addition
Subtraction
Word Problems
Unknown Numbers

MathFlare
Multiplication
MATH WORKBOOK
Grade 2
Step by Step Guide and Essential Practice with Answers
Multiply by 1 to 10
Commutative Property
Multiplication Drills
Fact Families

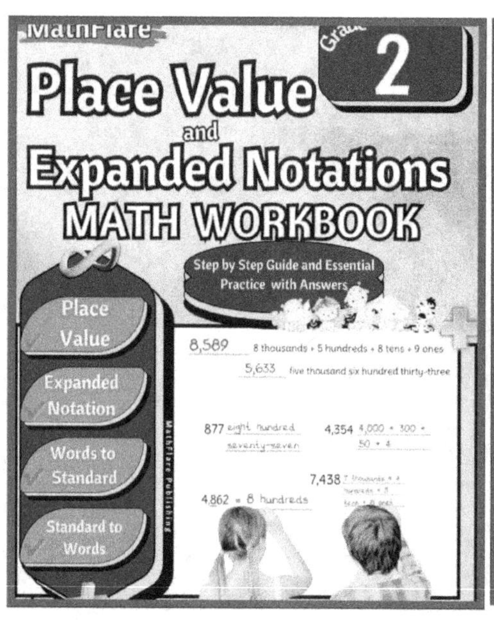
MathFlare
Grade 2
Place Value
and
Expanded Notations
MATH WORKBOOK
Step by Step Guide and Essential Practice with Answers
Place Value
Expanded Notation
Words to Standard
Standard to Words

MathFlare
Grade 2-3
Long
Division
MATH WORKBOOK
Step by Step Guide and Essential Practice with Answers
Basic Division
Long Divison
Division with Remainders
Answers Included

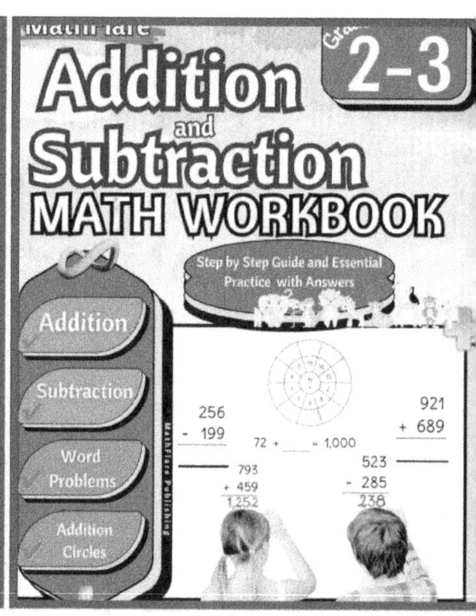
MathFlare
Grade 2-3
Addition
and
Subtraction
MATH WORKBOOK
Step by Step Guide and Essential Practice with Answers
Addition
Subtraction
Word Problems
Addition Circles

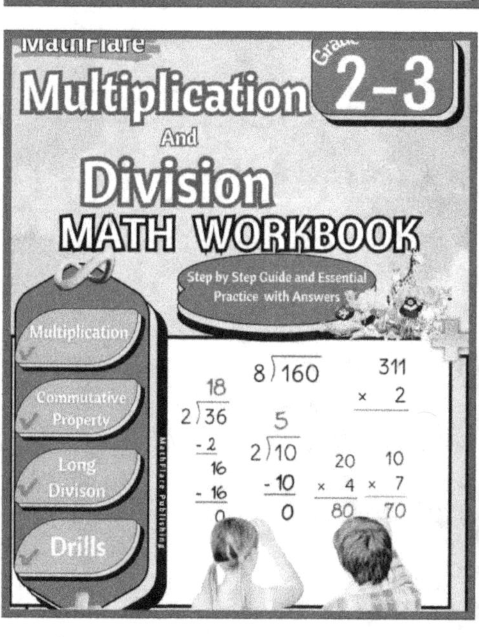
MathFlare
Grade 2-3
Multiplication
And
Division
MATH WORKBOOK
Step by Step Guide and Essential Practice with Answers
Multiplication
Commutative Property
Long Divison
Drills

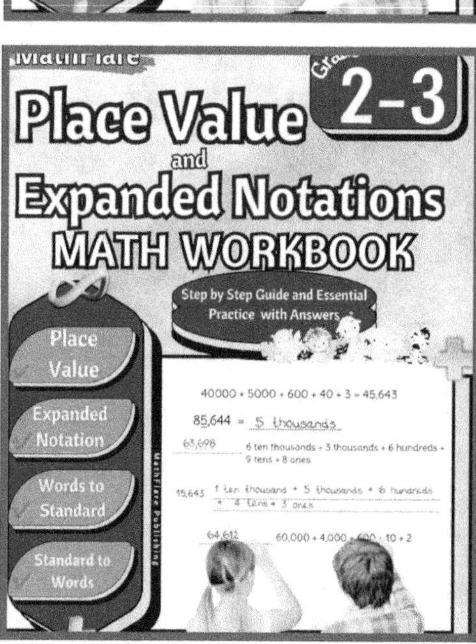
MathFlare
Grade 2-3
Place Value
and
Expanded Notations
MATH WORKBOOK
Step by Step Guide and Essential Practice with Answers
Place Value
Expanded Notation
Words to Standard
Standard to Words

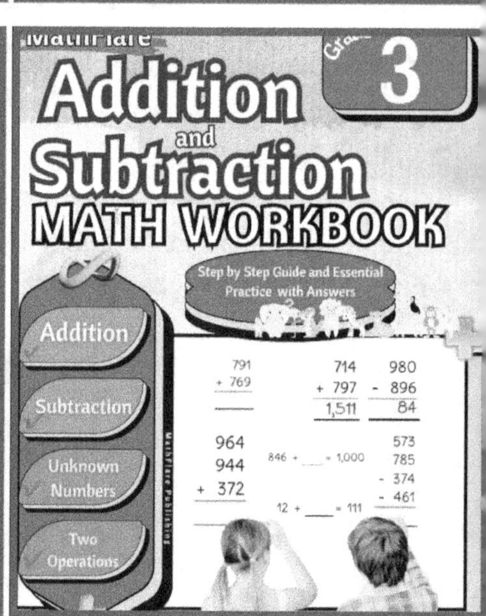
MathFlare
Grade 3
Addition
and
Subtraction
MATH WORKBOOK
Step by Step Guide and Essential Practice with Answers
Addition
Subtraction
Unknown Numbers
Two Operations

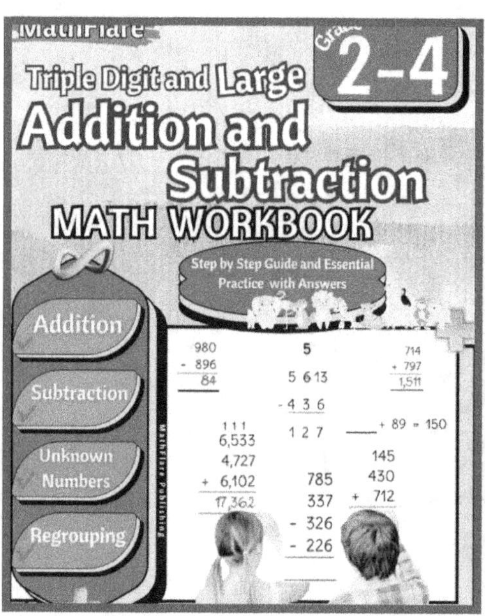
MathFlare
Grade 2-4
Triple Digit and Large
Addition and
Subtraction
MATH WORKBOOK
Step by Step Guide and Essential Practice with Answers
Addition
Subtraction
Unknown Numbers
Regrouping

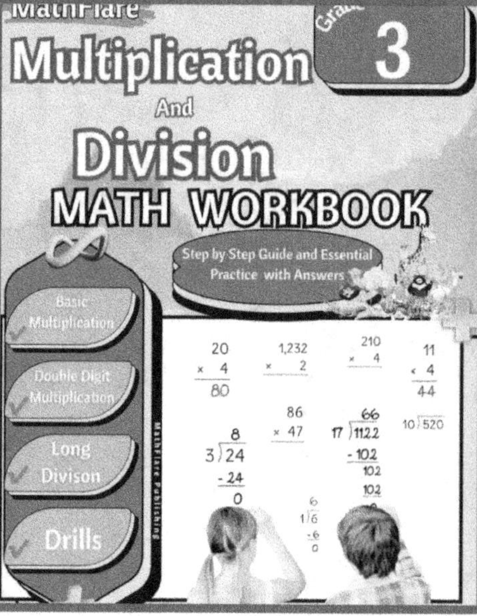
MathFlare
Grade 3
Multiplication
And
Division
MATH WORKBOOK
Step by Step Guide and Essential Practice with Answers
Basic Multiplication
Double Digit Multiplication
Long Divison
Drills

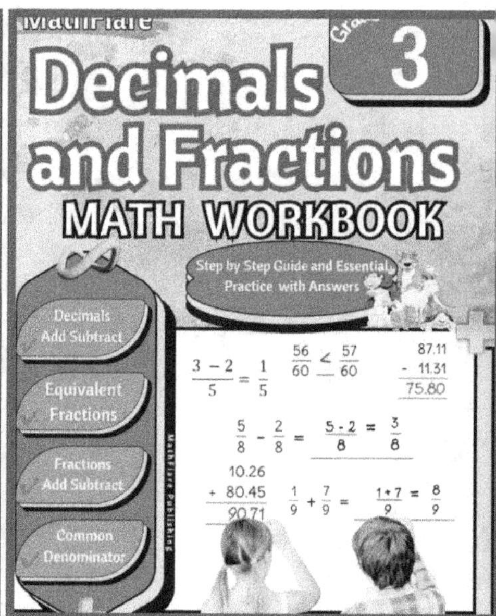
MathFlare
Grade 3
Decimals
and Fractions
MATH WORKBOOK
Step by Step Guide and Essential Practice with Answers
Decimals Add Subtract
Equivalent Fractions
Fractions Add Subtract
Common Denominator

www.ingramcontent.com/pod-product-compliance
Lightning Source LLC
Chambersburg PA
CBHW080942120726
48003CB00011B/3253